ALEXANDER POPE

ALEXANDER

𝔓𝔬𝔭𝔢

BY

BONAMY DOBRÉE

GREENWOOD PRESS, PUBLISHERS
NEW YORK

Originally published in 1951 by Sylvan Press Ltd.

Reprinted by permission
of Philosophical Library, Inc.

First Greenwood Reprinting 1969

SBN 8371-2459-X

PRINTED IN UNITED STATES OF AMERICA

TO

GEORGE SHERBURN

CONTENTS

PREFACE

IN writing a brief biography of a man so intricate as Pope, the biographer, besides omitting much, has to make up his mind on dubious points, and state his results. There is no room to argue the case, and I can only hope that my interpretation of certain incidents will not shock the informed.

With the older chroniclers as a background, from Spence onward, such as Ruffhead, Dr Johnson (still to be read), Carruthers and Leslie Stephen, not omitting C. W. Dilke's enlightening *Papers of a Critic*, I am chiefly indebted to *The Early Career of Alexander Pope* by Professor George Sherburn, that great authority, to whom I owe besides a far greater debt, for he has been more than kind in reading the greater part of my manuscript, and saving me from some of my grosser errors. All students of Pope owe gratitude to his scholarly work, as they must to Dr Edith Sitwell's intuitively sympathetic *Alexander Pope*, to the clear and perceptive presentation of Professor H. Kilburn Root in his *Poetical Life of Alexander Pope*, and to Professor R. H. Griffiths' masterly bibliography. No one interested in Pope can afford to miss the studies of the late Norman Ault, either his Introduction to *The Prose Works of Alexander Pope*, 1711–1720, or his *New Light on Pope*.

For appreciation of Pope's poetic qualities, the reader will find vivid interest in Professor Geoffrey Tillotson's brilliant *On the Poetry of Pope*, as he will again in his Introduction to his volume in the Twickenham Edition of Pope, *The Rape of the Lock, and other poems*. The volumes in this edition that have so far appeared, *The Dunciad* by Professor James Sutherland, and the *Imitations of Horace* by Professor John Butt, are admirable and indispensable. I have borrowed from all of these, without specific acknowledgement, as I have from Mr G. Wilson Knight's deeply illuminating chapter on Pope in *The Burning Oracle:* and I would like here to state my general indebtedness to these writers, who are at last putting us into a position to regard Pope rightly and generously.

B. D.

September, 1950

PROLOGUE

NOBODY has ever seen Pope plain. This is partly because
people either love or hate him so much that their view is
coloured one way or the other; but also because he often
took such extraordinary pains to cover his tracks, so enjoyed
making mysteries, and so often felt compelled to justify
himself, and draw flattering self-portraits. You can never be
sure whether you are looking at Pope as he was, or as he
would like you to see him, or as he would certainly detest
your doing.

That is one of the reasons why he is so fascinating. You
can feel he is a great man, besides being a great poet, but he
seems sometimes to be petty and spiteful: then suddenly he
is gentle and loyal. Sometimes he appears horribly mean,
and then again he is amazingly generous. He takes his part
in the ordinary concerns of literary and social life, but he is
agonizingly sensitive, tortured by his feelings. He had

enormous difficulties to overcome. His spirit was contained in 'a little tender and crazy carcase', and he was constantly in pain from headaches and rheumatism. Again, as a Catholic living just after the Revolution, he was in an uncertain position, and had few rights as a citizen. Therefore he is frequently on the defensive, and sometimes seems to twist and turn like a hunted animal trying to escape. But he has the courage to do what he wants to do, often desperately, and use his only weapon, his pen: and by God he does use it! People complained of his treatment of them because he hit them so much more shrewdly than they knew how to hit him. And since it was they who usually began, all that some of his earliest victims can do is to warn others: 'This creature is vicious; if you attack him he will bite'.

But whatever you may think of Pope, it is immensely exciting to go along with him through his densely packed career. Few men of letters offer lives crammed with so many sustained crises, pervaded with such continuous paradox. All that can be done in a short space is to fix the landmarks, to catch if we can a fleeting glimpse, a tone of voice, a gesture, to give momentary reality to the quivering sensibility which lies so shallow beneath the surface of the past as to seem ready to spring up before us. There is no need to judge. Moral reprobation at two hundred years is faintly ridiculous – if not suspect. Yet there is this to be asked: Is it likely that a man as treacherous and despicable as some of his biographers have made him out, could have been the lifelong friend of men outstanding in ability, terror or charm, such as Arbuthnot, Swift, Gay, and, yes, Bolingbroke, whose stature is far greater than is usually admitted? The difficulty with Pope is that he is still so alive, so vibrant, that it is hard not to be partisan. One must humbly try to be reasonable.

I

THE FORMATIVE YEARS

THE first vivid picture we get is that of a boy of about fourteen riding through the glades of Windsor Forest chattering eagerly with a man well over sixty. He is small and pale, fragile, and already not quite straight in the back, for during the past two years he has dallied far too intently over his reading and scribbling; but he has a frighteningly sensitive face, large wondering eyes, and an enchanting voice which will earn him the name of 'the little nightingale'. You might think that in this year of 1702, the pair would be discussing the recent accession of Queen Anne, which may affect the position of Catholics, about which the boy would be anxious. The senior man you might expect to be droning out political pieties, for he is Sir William Trumbull, a distinguished diplomat who has served at various Courts abroad, and lately been Secretary of State. But at present neither of them is at all interested in politics; what enthralls them, and what they are perpetually talking of, is poetry, particularly classical poetry, about which Sir William knows a great deal, and his young companion a great deal less than he thinks he ought to. But what he did know, and the way he knew it, keenly and intuitively, astonished and magnetized the old ambassador.

Yet the boy's education had been an unbalanced, scrappy sort of affair. 'God knows,' Pope was to say later, 'all the teaching I ever had . . . extended a very little way.' Still, it was far enough for him to be able to curl himself up in a great chair and brood over one book after another for gloriously endless hours, Homer and Virgil, Spenser, Milton and – at last – the incomparable Dryden, whose versification was a perpetual delight. He had seen Dryden. When he was at school at Mr Thomas Deane's near Hyde Park Corner, he had been taken, trembling with eagerness, to Will's coffee-house in Covent Garden, to catch a glimpse of the magnificent emperor of letters sitting in his corner, a little aloof. That was a vision he would never forget.

And if the memory set him musing about that school, he would remember that one of the good things about it had been the occasional slipping away to the theatre – and once the delight of concocting a scene out of Ogilby's translation of Homer, padded out with a few lines of his own, and getting Mr Deane's gardener to play the part of Ajax. It is true he hadn't learnt much there, he thought; but at least it was more than he would ever have picked up at the Twyford school he had been sent to when he was eight, under a grotesque headmaster upon whom he had written a lampoon. Outrageously, in his opinion, 'whipped and ill-used' for so natural a prank, his parents had mercifully swept him away from there at once. As he looked back, he felt he had imbibed most from the priest who called himself, with prudent evasiveness, either Banister or Taverner, and with whom he had read quite a deal of Latin and Greek before being lamentably entrusted to the man at Twyford.

At all events, here in the Forest it was delicious. Nobody worried him. There had indeed for a short time been another priest who had boringly kept his nose down to prosaic

Cicero, most absurdly, seeing that he was already translating away gaily from Homer and Statius. Now there was peace. He might, perhaps, be disturbed by his friendly Aunt Eliza, who had taught him to read, for though his mother was a great lady, she wasn't as happy as her sister at writing, or at spelling, in those days much a matter of taste. Poetry was hardly their province; but his father was something of a critic, although his books consisted chiefly of polemical theology. He would enjoy looking at his son's poetry, and if he liked a poem would say 'That is a very good rhyme,' and if he did not would tell him to 'turn' the verses better. It was when he was twelve, and they had just settled here, that he had composed for his father the lines 'On Solitude', which surely expressed what his father felt about coming to the Forest. They seemed to clinch his retirement: and if they were rather the sort of thing Horace might have written, they were none the worse for that. He would no doubt feel the same thing himself in due course; indeed he had imagined himself into feeling it when he wrote the final stanza:

> Thus, let me live, unseen, unknown,
> Thus, unlamented, let me die,
> Steal from the world, and not a stone,
> Tell where I lie.

imagined it so wholly, that he had believed it, and been moved by his belief. But first he was going to live the life of a poet, among men, have magnificent conversations, know everyone worth knowing, love and be loved – and write poetry, always write poetry.

It is rather in that way that Alexander Pope comes clearly into view soon after his father had settled down in the charming little country house at Binfield. The elder Alex-

ander Pope had wound up his business as linen-draper in
the Strand in 1688, soon after the boy had been born.The
Revolution had trumpetingly dispelled the brief dream of
Catholic   dominance,   making   rickety   the   position   of
Papists; and since at the age of forty-two he had made
enough to retire on, he acknowledged the new law for-
bidding Papists to live within ten miles of London by rent-
ing a house at Hammersmith, which was far enough away
to suggest good intentions. Then, while getting some teaching for his boy, he looked about for something more per-
manent, and deeper in the country, for a neighbourhood
where people were tolerant in religion, and, preferably,
rich in families that shared his faith. Himself a convert to
Rome – his father had been a Church of England parson –
he had lately married one of the Catholic Turners of York-
shire, a woman with the graciousness, competence, and
moral integrity associated with a decent county family,
together with considerable natural wit. Bearing an only
child in her later forties, she felt for her son a passionate
devotion which he unvaryingly returned; all that she asked
was the quiet deep enjoyment of a home among neighbours
who would not fret her. The Forest offered every promise.
And ready to be acquired from Charles Rackett, who had
married Mr Pope's daughter by a former marriage, and
lived at Bagshot only seven miles from it, was Whitehill
House, with fourteen acres, enclosed in the Manor of Binfield which was owned by Catholics: so there the family
moved some time in 1700. It was, however, the Protestant
Sir William Trumbull who was their nearest neighbour,
ever and anon strolling over to discuss 'hartichokes' with
the elder Mr Pope, and poetry with the younger. For the
boy it was intellectual salvation to have such a man to talk
to, since he had now virtually to educate himself; and

Trumbull's discursions on the classics, fortifying his own intuition and his appetite for English poetry, enabled him to achieve the desired end brilliantly – for his own purpose. To round it off, at fifteen he insisted on going to London to learn French and Italian. How he lived there, and with whom, we do not know; but we do know that after a few months he came back with a reading knowledge of both languages; and if to the end of his days he garbled French villainously in speech, and Italian he never spoke at all, that did not matter so long as he could enjoy the poetry and criticism of two more great literatures.

We see, of course, that he worked intemperately, at a tension far too high for a boy; and though he was not yet the pitiable physical wreck he was to become, it was from this time that he could date the beginning of what he later referred to as 'that long disease, my life'. His meagre frame, never much more than four foot six high, could not support the long vigils over books. He seems to have suffered from Pott's disease, a tubercular infection which later made him almost a cripple; already curvature of the spine was beginning to warp him. Soon, racked by nervous headaches, and in a mood of infantile self-pity and adolescent dramatization, he sat down to write farewell letters to 'some of his more particular friends' whom he thought would be affected by his early death. And in fact his illness might have proved fatal had it not been that among his correspondents was the Abbé Southcote, who did not intend to listen to any morbid nonsense, and sent down from London the brusque Dr Radcliffe, who liked telling suffering exquisites that there was nothing the matter with them – for which reason the Queen herself had ceased to be his patient. He sensibly advised less study and more riding; so horse exercise with Sir William Trumbull became part of Pope's routine.

Then, with the discontinuous suddenness of a dream, he appears flitting blithely about fashionable literary society in London, the wonder-youth of the elderly literati, who for the obvious genius in him could forgive – though younger sparks resented – 'that sort of awkwardness', which, he confessed, 'one always brings up at first out of the country'. Beautifully deferential, we may suppose, after the manner of an apprentice potentially equal to his masters, or more, he seems to have charmed them completely. Earliest among them was Wycherley, the battered old Restoration beau living on his portentous prestige as a comedy writer, and who with such inconceivable rashness wheedled Pope into 'mending' his atrocious lyrics for him. Dazzled by a pastoral or two that Pope showed him, or perhaps read to him in his enchanting voice, he passed them to to Walsh, who demanded to meet the young poet; and so, by a kind of snow-ball process one figure after another added itself. It is as though the older men who might have been poets, or better poets than they actually were, saw in this extra-ordinary youth someone who would realize all that they had missed, and enjoyed that kind of vicarious living in the young not uncommon with the frustrated ageing. They encouraged Pope, and he never forgot this early goodwill. Some thirty years later he was to sing in the *Prologue to the Satires:*

> Granville the polite
> And knowing Walsh, would tell me I could write;
> Well-natur'd Garth inflam'd with early praise,
> And Congreve lov'd, and Swift endur'd my Lays;
> The courtly Talbot, Somers, Sheffield read,
> E'en mitred Rochester would nod the head . . .

a galaxy enough to flush any young poet with a sense of pre-cocious success. The list does not include all his well-wishers;

he omits, for instance, not only Wycherley, but the old rake
Henry Cromwell, who, though shining with all the glamour
of the man of the world, could yet talk intelligently about
poetry, and emancipate a youth in the free adult realm by
treating him as an equal.

'Knowing' Walsh! There is no glamour about the name
now, and the adjective – others are showered in the *Essay
on Criticism* – has ceased to be complimentary. But in 1705
they referred to a well-known Member of Parliament of
about forty-two, one of those brilliant amateurs of letters
who expend themselves chiefly in talk. His poems seem to
us boring trifles, 'flimsy and frigid', but he was immensely
knowledgeable about poetry; and after all Dryden had called
him 'without flattery . . . the best critic of our nation'. To
Pope he made the notorious remark 'that there was one way
left of excelling: for though we had several great poets, we
never had one great poet that was correct; and he desired
me to make that my study and my aim.' Correctness! the
word has done Pope's reputation as a poet more damage
than any other epithet conceivable. It seems to imply cold-
ness, starch in approaching the passions, a hacking about of
the most effulgent emotions to make them fit a rigid metre,
applying a mean arithmetical standard dreary enough to
make any muse droop despondently. As though you could
write poetry by rule! But of course, whatever the well-
meaning Walsh hoped to convey, the above is precisely
what Pope did not mean by correctness. The emotions came
first with him – the exquisite sense of the outer world,
burning rage, icy scorn more searing than fire, the piercing
sweetness of nostalgia, or the calm warmth of friendship;
'correctness' meant the passionate search for, the triumphant
finding of, the exact words, rhythms, vowel-sounds, diction
and texture – in fact the right form and heat and colour to

make the emotion glow on the face of the poem itself and vibrate in the reader's heart. Correctness meant really knowing your job, knowing it as no English poet had known it before; it meant an infinity of labour, immense knowledge, constant practice and revision and re-writing. You might always, of course, and none knew it better than he, 'snatch a grace beyond the reach of art'; that is what the gods sometimes send to those who labour. But 'to write well, lastingly well, immortally well, must one not leave father and mother and cleave unto the Muse?' he wrote to Bolingbroke some twenty years later. A truth every poet knows, and Pope came to it early. It was what the ideal of 'correctness' had made him learn. He called it 'perfection', and it became his lodestar and his bane.

The Fledgling

Pope, then, had early found a group of influential patron-friends prepared to back him; and now, daily increasing in social poise, he felt he could as by right frequent Will's, and foregather with the remnants of the Dryden coterie. Meanwhile the rumour of his eclogues grew, till on April 20th, 1706, the at once soundest and most enterprising publisher in London wrote to him:

> Sir,—I have lately seen a Pastoral of yours in Mr Walsh's and Mr Congreve's hands, which is extremely fine, and is generally approved by the best judges in poetry. . . . If you design your poem for the press, no person shall be more careful in the printing of it, nor no one can give greater encouragement to it than, sir, your, &c.
>
> JACOB TONSON

A letter to make any young man's heart leap for joy – and Pope was a mere boy of eighteen! But not so fast; one pastoral by itself would not do; there were to be four eclogues, one for each season, and such as were written by this date would need infinite burnishing, since 'correctness' was to be a shining quality from the start.

So, with this propitious beginning, Pope went back to the Forest, to be visited now and again by some of his new friends, and himself going off in 1707 to stay with Walsh at his place of Abberley in Worcestershire. There he could discuss poetry without interruption, and no doubt more rigorously than was possible with Trumbull. While at home he extended his circle of acquaintance, especially among the Catholic folk centred about Anthony Englefield at White-knights, some nine miles from Binfield: there he met John Caryll of Ladyholt, who was so long to be a sort of theological barometer warning Pope when storms might gather; and, more momentously still, Englefield's granddaughters, Teresa and Martha (or 'Patty') Blount, who lived not far away at Mapledurham. Against this background of quiet, architecturally decorous houses set in fragrant gardens still at that time Italianate and formal, he developed his emotional side, his heart warming first to Teresa, then to Martha Blount, to whom he gave all the trembling devotion of first adolescent love. And all the while he was working, reading, pondering every word he had written, and engaging with his literary friends in what we can only call 'epistolary correspondence', so stilted does the manner seem to us, though occasionally relieved by a little touch of flippant impropriety, to offset the atmosphere of religious devoutness which sometimes weighed a little heavily on the house. He was feeling outwards, while he waited for emancipation.

At last, on May 2nd, 1709, there was issued the sixth volume of Tonson's *Poetical Miscellanies*, which displayed early in the book some pastorals of a protégé of Addison's, Ambrose Philips, and at the end, Pope's, together with his translations of a tale of Chaucer and a scrap of Homer. However, Pope's first public appearance as a poet caused no wild excitement. The Homer was well enough, and it was always entertaining to read in modern idiom one of Chaucer's racily improper stories: and as for the eclogues, well, after all, why should anyone get more than languidly interested in these faint classical echoes? It was only those really sensitive to poetry (always few) who could respond to the exquisite workmanship in these things. They saw that here was something very startling by way of juvenilia. We of to-day would most likely not read them at all if Pope had written nothing further, yet they have a certain charm anyone can enjoy, even if they cannot taste the uncanny precocious skill. Artificial? Why, of course. What else should they be? They were precisely the same sort of thing as Dresden shepherds and shepherdesses. On those terms we can like them; and at least one passage from the second eclogue is familiar to most of us as the Handelian song, 'Where'er you walk'. Serious and passionate? Why, no; not with respect to the life supposedly represented, but with respect to poetry, a thousand times yes. And that, in a young poet, is what matters.

But long before these things were published, Pope was busy on his next very considerable work, *An Essay on Criticism*, which arose out of his reading, and his colloquies with Walsh, who, however, had died in 1708, while the poem was embryonic. It took three years to mature, and in the meantime Pope engaged in the oddest ritual dance with Wycherley. It will be remembered that soon after the old dramatist met Pope, he had asked the boy – for he was then no more – to help him improve his occasional verses – madrigals as he chose to call them. Only a very innocent youth would have accepted the task, but the idea must have been irresistibly flattering: here, asking for his help, was Wycherley, a great man, with more of 'the nobleman look' than Pope ever saw, and a very likeable person arrayed in the glamour of a literary hero of the last age. So Pope enthusiastically took the job in hand; far too enthusiastically, because to make anything at all out of Wycherley's limping verse meant such drastic alterations as to cut the would-be poet to the quick. Besides, the old man's memory was treacherous in the extreme; he never noticed when he repeated himself, and was beautifully unconscious of his blatant cribbing from the most familiar classics. Pope was torn between his craftsman's conscience and his real respect for the decaying dramatist. Thus the published correspondence between the two achieves delicate high comedy; the whole thing is at once absurd and touching. We find Pope being a little too outspoken, guilty of no 'cruel charity', and Wycherley itching to burst out indignantly, but realizing that after all this was just the treatment he had begged for. So he makes a courtly bow, writing: 'Now as for what you call freedom with me, which you desire me to forgive, you may be assured that I would not forgive you unless you did use it.' We find them sparring in their elegant formal letters, human irritation breaking through the convention of extravagant compliment. But though we know that when it was all over Pope would not have dedicated a poem to Wycherley as he had one of the eclogues, nor Wycherley have responded with commendatory lines, both came bravely out of the ordeal. There was, naturally, a cooling, but no open rupture, no rancour, no uneasiness; they remained on friendly social terms, and late in 1715, Pope, himself now a considerable figure, twice went to see the old man when he was dying.

When, on May 15th, 1711, *An Essay on Criticism* at last came out, Pope must have expected more immediate praise than he got; for if it was not the sort of thing to cause a rush to the booksellers, at least the established men of letters who admired it might have spoken up more loudly. The thoughts, to be sure, were not very new, nor did Pope ever pretend they were; yet he could justly claim that the poem very neatly summed up the neo-classical position everybody accepted. Apart from that, however, the whole heavy matter was so lightly handled, made to sparkle so gaily as the statements swung briskly along to their appointed end in the couplet, that once known it became a mine of popular tags. We think off-hand of such well-worn – and often slightly misquoted – phrases as:

> A little learning is a dangerous thing . . .

or,

> To err is human, to forgive divine . . .

or again,

> For fools rush in where angels fear to tread . . .

and the passages throb expressively with words handled to suggest the sense by the sound, modulating from the turgid to a lovely lilt as in:

> When Ajax strives some rock's vast weight to throw,
> The line too labours, and the words move slow;
> Not so, when Swift Camilla scours the plain,
> Flies o'er the unbending corn, and skims along the main.

Salted as it was with a few lively hits, Pope could not be blamed for hoping that it would at once be seized on as something delightful to read. But for the moment it passed disappointingly unnoticed.

By most people, that is, but not by John Dennis, whose attention it a little rudely invited. Dennis was an unfortunate man, a better critic than anyone would give him credit for, irascible since failure had soured him, and beginning to feel that he was the victim of a literary conspiracy. A play of his, *Appius and Virginia*, had lately fallen as flat as his others, and knowing himself to be more competent than his critics he was apt to explode when contradicted. Already reputed cantankerous, rising young writers tended to bait him; so when he read:

> Fear not the anger of the wise to raise;
> Those best can bear reproof who merit praise.
> 'Twere well might critics still this freedom take,
> But Appius reddens at each word you speak,
> And stares tremendous with a threatening eye,
> Like some fierce tyrant in old tapestry . . .

he found the allusion only too clear, especially as it was notorious that his favourite adjective was 'tremendous'. He flared up into almost maniacal rage, and indeed there was some excuse for him. The authorship of the anonymous poem was an open secret, and, judged impartially, such a remark coming from a young author of twenty-three to a veteran of fifty-five or so, who had done honourable service in the critical wars, was monstrously impertinent. Who, after all, Dennis with some justice thought, was this young upstart to make these remarks? He had been loudly heralded, but what had he produced apart from some 'amorous pastoral madrigals', which might be harmonious but were empty of passion; and passion was what Dennis as a good Miltonian demanded. And this *Essay*, he fumed, leaky with inconsistencies, muddled . . . an utterly unprovoked attack . . . not on his opinions, either, but on his person . . . skulking behind anonymity, a trick he, Dennis, had never been guilty of. He would make the conceited little animal writhe.

We cannot but sympathize: yet nothing can excuse the utter brutality of his retort, not even the crudeness of an age which our more queasy one finds it hard to understand, that he published on June 20th as *Reflections, Critical and*

Satyrical, upon a late Rhapsody called an Essay upon Criticism: for besides relentlessly savaging the Essay, he gibed at Pope's physique, flaying alive the most sensitive of beings. Pope was displayed as 'a squab, short Gentleman . . . and the very bow of the God of Love', the world being warned that 'as there is no creature in Nature so venemous, there is nothing so stupid and impotent as a hunch-backed Toad': and, Dennis added, much as Pope might revel in extolling the ancients, had he been born of Grecian parents, 'his life would have been no longer than that of one of his Poems, the Life of half a Day'. Mercifully the publisher showed Pope this outrageous document before releasing it to the eyes of malice, so that Pope was able to evade the derisive whispers and pitying glances of the coffee-houses, and retire to the country to lick his wounds. He put up a bold front, pretended a careless indifference, and after eighteen months was able to tell Caryll that the book had made him 'very heartily merry in two minutes' time'.

Nevertheless it had been a hideous blow, in a sense a mortally wounding one, because it had devastatingly revealed to him that the loveliest of all human relationships would be eternally denied him. We find him a little later referring to himself as 'the little Alexander the women laugh at', and he will one day write to the young ladies at Mapledurham: 'I have heard, indeed, of women that have had a kindness for men of my make', and there is a feeling of despair about both the phrases. But if the horror caused a little drop of venom to be distilled into some of his later work, what is remarkable and admirable is Pope's plucky resilience, his refusal to lie down and whimper: if self-justification is the leitmotiv running through a good many of his poems, there is little self-pity in the mature man: and

in the summer or early autumn he got to work on one of the
gayest and most perfect of all his works, *The Rape of the
Lock*. The theme, a delightful one, was suggested by Caryll,
coming to the rescue as so many friends did at this cruel
moment. It arose out of a prank, a 'frolic of gallantry',
played in Catholic high society by Lord Petre, who snipped
off one of the irresistible curls which adorned the nape of
Miss Arabella Fermor's neck. A little bickering had ensued
between the families, and it occurred to Caryll, who was
related to Petre, that a humorous treatment of the incident
by a Catholic poet might restore good temper. Pope seized
blithely on the idea – among the things to be restored might
also be his self-esteem – and in a miraculously short time (he
said a fortnight), produced a charming little mock-heroic
poem in two cantos, a piece full of good-nature, fun, and
laughter, with a good deal more which only people alive to
the implications of first-rate poetry would notice or care for.
For the first time, too, you feel that Pope is really singing;
he is on top of his medium. At all events, Miss Fermor
approved the poem, had copies made and passed round, and
everybody was pleased except the original of Sir Plume, who
was, to be sure, made out an ass, and can be excused for
'blustering'. (Pope never could see why people minded his
laughing at them so long as his laughter was friendly.) The
poem, in short, was entirely successful, and Pope could
preen himself happily – until it was published, when the
comments of fools made Miss Fermor uneasy.

But if Caryll was ready to comfort him with respect to
the *Essay* so far as Dennis's attack went, and encouraged
him over *The Rape of the Lock*, he was not for a moment
going to waver in his role of Pope's theological conscience,
and there were some verses in the *Essay* that needed explaining. There was, for instance, the phrase 'dull be-

lievers'; and something acid about the monks finishing the
destruction of culture that the Goths had begun; and again
an ambiguous – to say the least of it – remark about Eras-
mus, not quite to the taste of the orthodox. At first Pope,
with his natural hunted animal's instinct for evasion,
funked the issue; it was due to misreading, and could all be
accounted for by punctuation. But Caryll, supported, it
seems likely, by Southcote, insisted that no misreading
could palliate:

> . . . wit, like faith, by each man is apply'd
> To one small sect, and all are damn'd beside;

and then Pope, driven into a corner, stuck to his guns. Was
it any service to their Church, he asked Caryll, to claim that
it had always been perfect? It was surely far better 'openly
to expose our detestation and scorn' of all those pious frauds
which merely give rise to scandal: it was the 'uncharitable
assertion' that Catholics alone could hope for salvation that
had made their religion a 'scarecrow' to others. And besides,
he continued, 'in our own church we must again subdivide,
and the Jansenist is damned by the Jesuit, the Jesuit by the
Jansenist, the strict Scotist by the Thomist, etc.' Living in
the circles that he did, it argues a good deal of moral courage on Pope's part to have made this sort of statement: but
courage, physical as well as moral, was one of Pope's great
virtues.

This passage of arms exhibits also a second of his great
virtues, tolerance and hatred of bigotry, coupled as it often
is not, with sensibility for the religious feelings of others.
He was, in fact, as near as does not matter, a Deist –
Chesterfield's testimony is good enough for that – and the
fervent will no doubt accuse him of indifferentism: yet some
sort of basic faith – or was it loyalty? – prevented him from

ever abjuring the religion he was brought up in. When his father died, and Bishop Atterbury suggested that there was now no reason why he should not become a convert to the Anglican Church and obtain preferment, Pope replied that his mother would find 'such a separation more grievous than any other'; and, he added, ' I mean as well in the religion I now profess, as I can possibly ever do in another.' Though Pope may not have been an orthodox Christian, that he was a religious man no student of either his work or his life can doubt: at least he believed profoundly in certain ethical values.

These do not at once emerge – they were to be superbly stated in his final phase – for such values have to be patiently carved out in living; and before arriving at them Pope was to lead, in the first instance, the life of the brilliant young poet about town and in country houses. For some years this was to be an extremely busy one, full of rattle and noise and controversy, as well as of deep emotion and the writing of the more glowing poetry of the first phase, in which satire was only an occasional visitor. Much of what happened to Pope as a man is necessarily obscure, but it was in this autumn of 1711 that emerged the fully-feeling man, aware of the depth of his sensibility at the same time that he became conscious of how good a poet he was. Possibly the tremendous shock of the blow dealt him by Dennis – the result of riding a little too cock-a-whoop on his early successes – was his first really deepening experience, and it is in the next year or two that we find him falling in love, and interesting himself in the unlucky fate of two women whom he thought wronged, namely a Mrs Weston, and whoever it was that may have been the 'unfortunate lady' of a later elegy – possibly Mrs Cope (if indeed, the lady wa s not purely imaginary). All was charming and foolish and impetuous in these oddly chivalrous championships, Pope's impulsive knight-errantry being matched only by his ignorance of how things happen in the world; but at all events the incidents taught Pope a great deal, luckily not so much as to prevent him from acting impetuously on many occasions later in his life, though enough to suggest that man did not stand quite so near the angels as he seems to have supposed.

That he now fell in love with Martha Blount, with a devoted, delicate and lasting passion, seems plain enough; and it may be that it was the sheer kindliness he read in her notoriously blue eyes that made him regard her always as an encouragement, a stay and a refuge. In common with numerous others in that difficult summer, she conspired to salve the wound caused by Dennis: Caryll, we have seen, rushed to the rescue, Cromwell came to stay at Binfield, Wycherley resumed a correspondence that had been broken off, and altogether Pope – you can feel it in his letters – was leading an intense personal life.

Moreover, fresh fields of literature opened up. Steele, so far no more than a literary acquaintance, invited him to write a poem to be set to music by the composer Clayton, a request which brought forth the 'Ode to Music', now an unduly slighted piece. Also, at the end of the year *The Spectator* favourably noticed the hitherto neglected *Essay on Criticism*, in a paper which might be regarded as a reply to Dennis, though the reviewer deplored the inclusion in the poem of a few remarks which might give offence. Pope, though he protested that he couldn't see what remarks could possibly give offence, wrote to thank Steele, who then divulged that the article had been written by Addison, so paving the way for an introduction to the king of popular letters. Thus further encouraged, Pope drove ahead with his work, preparing for publication (since so many copies had got about, and piracy threatened) the poem about Miss Arabella Fermor's misadventure: in the spring he published in a collection of *Ovid's Epistles* garnered by Tonson, a translation of *Sappho to Phaon*, beautifully done, heavy with emotion; and *The Spectator* of May 14th, 1712, offered his parents his *Messiah*, founded on Virgil's *Pollio*, which much comforted them, as they were beginning to fear that the Christian was being lost in the poet. A week later Lintot's *Miscellaneous Poems and Translations* contained further pieces by Pope, notably the first version of *The Rape of the Lock*, and an epistle 'To a Young Lady with the Works of Voiture'. This last is at once light and serious, and if in isolation it lacks interest, to anyone knowing the background it reads by no means flatly; for we see why he hopes that his life will be a gay innocent farce, why he suggests to the Young Lady – probably Miss Blount – that she would be wise to remain unmarried, and why he says that if she does marry she must base her happiness on good humour, and not on her 'now resistless charms'. To anyone behind the scenes the poem is tender and touching, to others it must seem a little too obviously moralistic. It was not the fashion in those days for poets to expose their hearts on publicly flaunted sleeves.

Covered up as they were, the stresses of the last twelve months, together with the exhausting work of poetic creation, told all the more on Pope's health. He was not well in the spring, and in early winter he describes himself as 'confined to a narrow closet, lolling on an armchair, nodding away my days over a fire'. But before long he is back in London – perhaps to escape the feminine censures showered upon him after his unwarranted if well-meant interference in the Weston affair – living with Charles Jervas, the painter. Pope had for some years dabbled in painting, and though he threw away most of his work (which consisted mainly of copies), such as 'three Swifts . . . two Lady Bridgewaters, a Duchess of Montague, half a dozen earls, and one Knight of the Garter', as he told Gay in August 1713, the discipline no doubt sharpened his already acute visual perception, and organized his eager response to colour.

These were brilliantly exemplified in the poem *Windsor Forest*, with which he opened his new campaign in London early in 1713. Begun as a descriptive 'place' poem, it followed previous models, and carried all the usual paraphernalia – such themes as the beauty of retirement, classical allusion, historical reference, and so on: but it has great merits, and even now strikes freshly because Pope really did love the Forest where he lived, and had eyes to see it. Companioned by his dog, 'a little one, a lean one, and none of the finest shaped' (since "'tis likeness that begets affection'), he would wander about the walks, the 'bowers and grottoes', impressing the forms and colours deeply upon his mind, noting where, for instance,

> . . . interspers'd in Lawns and op'ning Glades,
> Thin Trees arise, that shun each others' Shades.

And at the end of 1712, still clinging a little to his early patrons, he showed the poem, already perhaps in proof, to Granville, now Lord Lansdowne, made a peer to ensure the passage of the Tory Peace of Utrecht through the House of Lords: and Lansdowne suggested that Pope should make the poem glorify the peace, the country being heartily sick of the ten years' war. It would not need much alteration to the work, merely such details as a new invocation to Granville; and if here and there it involved a disastrous enough couplet, such as:

> At length great Anna said: 'Let discord cease!'
> She said, the world obey'd, and all was peace!

at least it caused Pope to write a magnificent ending. Thus he added one of the loveliest bits of his poetry, in singing a Utopian vision of England as the beneficent bestower of peace and prosperity upon the world. It is patriotic poetry at its best, free of any trace of jingoism, establishing the Thames as the source from which all good things should flow out to humanity:

> The time shall come, when free as seas or wind,
> Unbounded *Thames* shall flow for all mankind,
> Whole nations enter with each swelling tide,
> And Seas but join the regions they divide;
> Earth's distant ends our glory shall behold,
> And the new world launch forth to seek the old.
> Then ships of uncouth form shall stem the tide,
> And feather'd people crowd my wealthy side,
> Whose naked youth and painted chiefs admire
> Our speech, our colour, and our strange attire!
> Oh stretch thy reign, fair Peace! from shore to shore,
> Till conquest cease, and slav'ry be no more;
> Till the freed *Indians* in their native groves
> Reap their own fruits, and woo their sable loves,
> *Peru* once more a race of Kings behold,
> And other *Mexico's* be roof'd with gold.

Absurd? Possibly: but that is the sort of absurdity without which men cannot live – and besides, the vision came very nearly true. Perhaps the effect of the poem was a little marred by the publication, when Pope was still a few weeks short of his final polishing, of a poem by Thomas Tickell *On the Prospect of Peace;* but it did not make much difference. If Pope had the bother of altering one or two of his expressions so as to avoid the charge of plagiarism, Tickell's poem would remove any sense of party politics, since he was an Addisonian Whig. From the point of view of Pope's development the work was an advance: he was taking in more ground.

III

Skirmishes

But if the year was important for Pope's literary growth, it was still more so for his literary relationships. Now a fully-fledged author, flying alone, no longer under the wing of older protectors, he had to make choices, not only in the high fields of poetry where they can be made cleanly without shameful compromises, but in the hurly-burly of literary rivalry in a period where political tensions were highly charged, and it was impossible not to take sides. Complex by nature, as a man of his sensibility and intellectual power must inevitably be, his circumstances, physical and religious, made him a bundle of exaggerated intricacy. He was that sort of being who in so far as he is an artist contains in himself more of the divine than any other kind of human being: but in so far as he was a social creature, Pope was far from being divine. Moreover in his youth he saw no point in being more divine than other people. So what strikes us about him in these years is his feverish nervous energy, his intense spiritual vitality: but, living as he did, among and at the level of people of great physical as well as moral force, in this sense he lived always a little beyond his means, so that at times his behaviour appears to us, as it did to his contemporaries, over-strained. Some of his actions seem like

nervous adjustments, attempts to equal in displays of animal
vitality the rough-and-tumble men of affairs in council
chamber or tavern. In the end it told on him. What he did
may have been imprudent, yet we cannot help admiring
the brilliant activities of what we might call his spendthrift
days.

He was, we have seen, being drawn into the circle of
'Buttonians', that is, the group of writers headed by
Addison throning it at Button's coffee-house, the rising
centre of literary interest. Addison was always ready to
accept disciples, provided they were adoring enough, and
Pope seemed to be shaping nicely. In this early part of 1713
Addison was in the throes of bringing forth his great tragedy
of *Cato*, with such agonized birth-pangs as demanded an
inordinate amount of midwifery. Suppose it should be a
failure! a prospect unbearable to Addison. It had been hard
work to induce him to finish the play at all: it was only when
Hughes, a very minor poet, threatened to do it for him, that
he drove himself to the perilous labour. Almost everybody
was consulted about it, even Pope. Then there was the
political danger. The play, with its ringing declarations
about liberty might, from a Whig, be taken as a Whig manifesto, which would never do, since the Tories were in power.
Still, the prologue might be written by a Tory, and then, to
even things up and save recriminations, the epilogue could
safely be given to a Whig. Garth would do the latter very
well, and as for the prologue, why not Pope? Though he
repudiated party allegiance, that might be all the better, for
if *Windsor Forest* did not prove him a Tory, no Catholic
could be presumed to be a Whig. So Pope it was who turned
out the prologue, cleverly explaining why the play had so
little love interest: 'In pitying love we but our weakness
show' he stated, thus flaunting fashionable taste. And, if the

apostrophe 'Britons arise . . . ' might be taken as inciting to rebellion, it was easy to turn the phrase to 'Britons attend . . . '

Every care was taken to make the play go, and unheard of sums were spent on the production. Steele packed the house with adherents of Addison, who, supported by burgundy and a few friends, shivered and sweated in a box, on tenter-hooks for the result. He need not have been afraid. The Tories were so eager to at least equal their rivals as sup-porters of liberty, that they out-Whigged the Whigs in applause in the passages that might – though only in pre-judiced minds – have seemed to hint a reflection on Tory policy: the drama was thus assured of success quite apart from its merits as a play. Addison, naturally, was filled with 'complacent satisfaction' as he would have put it; and since Pope had a little contributed to the triumph (he had found himself 'clapped into a staunch Whig' as he told Caryll), the young poet was made to feel one of the fortunate who could bask in the Buttonian climate. He might ask Addison's advice, and did so with respect to the re-writing of *The Rape of the Lock*, the two cantos to be swelled to five by the addition of the supernatural 'machinery' which would make the mock epic more delightfully complete. There would also be a disarming dedication to Miss Fermor, to salve all scratches. Addison advised him against any additions: the little poem was perfect as it was, it would be a pity to spoil it. Typically Addisonian advice! He was a born 'better not' man, averse from taking any risk that could by any means be avoided. Caution personified gave the honest answer – yet it was to be remembered against him.

But if at this time Pope was friendly with Addison, he had reason to be offended with the Addison clique – the 'little Senate', the Buttonians – especially by a series of papers appearing in *The Guardian*, the journal which had succeeded *The Spectator*. He had all the more reason to be annoyed as he himself contributed to and otherwise helped in this new venture, which was run almost entirely by Steele, with whom he was always on the best of terms. These articles treated – not very originally – of pastoral poetry; and again and again they praised the eclogues of Philips while totally ignoring Pope's. This had happened in earlier pamphlets and poems, whose readers had been assured, as they were again here, that the great pastoral poets of the world were Theocritus, Virgil, Spenser, and – the tall, the elegant, the foppish Ambrose Philips. It really was intolerable! So Pope himself composed yet another essay on pastoral poetry (*Guardian* 40), calmly, judicially, with a bland assumption of complete fairness, comparing Philips's with his own. By only a little exaggerating the theories on which the earlier articles were based, and again by only a little exaggerating the praise already given to Philips, the article quite plausibly led to the conclusion that Philips, at least as far as pastoral writing went, was not only equal to, but 'excelled both Theocritus and Virgil'. Pope, as was clear, could not approach the perfect simplicity of Philips, but 'deviated into downright poetry'. At that point even the most spellbound admirer of Philips would begin to see: whereas those who already felt that Philips was after all a little namby-pamby (though that name was not given him till later), could follow with huge and growing delight the destruction not of Philips alone but also of the rather solemn theorizing of the earlier articles – which were, after all, merely being followed out to their logical conclusion. All Philips's most obvious absurdities were praised, especially, towards the end, his 'beautiful rusticity', Pope rapturously quoting:

> O woful day! O day of woe, quoth he,
> And woful I, who live the day to see.

adding: 'That simplicity of diction, the melancholy flowing of the numbers, the solemnity of the sound, and the easy turn of the words, in this dirge . . . are extremely elegant.'

The whole is a superb piece of light irony we can happily chuckle over even now: it is balanced, it is good-tempered, and it is sound criticism on purely literary grounds. Pope, naturally, wanted to destroy not only Philips, but the sludge, as he thought it, that Philips, together with Addison and the Buttonians, put forward as poetry. We of to-day might think the attack a little cruel, but after all it was nothing to the libellous vituperation which was the normal form of adverse criticism in those days. Moreover for Pope bad writing was the evil thing; it was immoral; it struck at the roots of society and of all decent behaviour. He knew that art mattered enormously, and that to debase poetry is far worse than to debase the coinage, for whereas with the latter you are merely altering the price of material things, if you debase art you sully all spiritual values. At any rate the whole performance was perfectly fair and legitimate. But Philips was furious, for it is hard to bear placidly being made to look ridiculous. It is doubtful whether he really did hang up a whip at Button's and swear to chastise Pope should he appear, but certainly he and the rest of the little Senate seethed with anger. Except for Steele, who stoutly protested that he had been taken in; the paper had been thrust anonymously into the *Guardian* office, and reading it roughly he had thought it was meant to praise the admirable Ambrose; he was very sorry, but . . . The truth was, he did not much love these upstarts, who, with their adulation, were sapping the moral foundations of his old friend Addison. He was impatiently jealous of them, of Philips

now, and later of Tickell, who had written the articles on
the pastoral – though it is doubtful if even Steele knew that;
certainly nobody else did. Or did Addison? How much the
latter resented the attack on Philips is not known; he was
probably not very easy about it, and it would not have made
him feel any the warmer towards Pope, who was, perhaps,
not going to be so devoted a member of his clique as he had
hoped.

Still, the young poet was shortly going to rally to the
defence of the older one against the egregious Dennis, who
unable any longer to bottle up his rage at the success of
Cato – though for a fortnight or so he tried desperately hard
– burst out with *Remarks upon Cato, A Tragedy*, egged on,
he said, by his friends, and not discouraged by his publisher
Lintot. He was profoundly irritated because he saw that the
play was successful not as art but as politics; having a high
view of the drama, and being an honourable critic, he could
not bear to see a lame thing puffed as though it were a
masterpiece. He therefore made a thoroughgoing swinge-
ing attack, in which he declared that Addison had made
Cato out an oaf 'who rashly dy'd by his own Hands, when
there was no Necessity for Dying,' and in general made out
the hero to be a traitor to the very causes for which he was
supposed to stand as a splendid and timely exemplar. And
after a terrible, and by no means brief tirade, he concluded
that 'this Author has found out the Secret to make his
Tragedy highly improbable, without making it wonderful,
and to make parts of it highly incredible, without being in
the least entertaining.' It was certainly slashing; but it is
hardly for posterity to object, since it has accepted Dennis's
judgement, rather too readily indeed, for the play is by no
means so dull or unactable as everybody for at least a
hundred and fifty years has glibly repeated. But Addison's

little Senate at Button's was deeply shocked, not to say
tumultuous with rage against Dennis's raging, especially as
there was an insidious suggestion in the *Remarks upon Cato*
that if Addison had really believed in his play, he need not
have been so careful to make advances to the Tory digni-
taries, so watchful to pack the house!

However right or wrong the outburst may have been, it
gave Pope his chance. It had, of course, been beneath his
wounded dignity to answer Dennis's disproportionately
rough attack on the *Essay upon Criticism* (though it has
been argued that an anonymous pamphlet – *The Critical
Specimen* of 1711 is his), just as it was far below Addison's
bolstered pose of rectitude to take any notice. But what objection could there be against Pope retorting on Addison's
behalf? Addison, however, refused all offers of help, thinking, no doubt, least said soonest forgotten – and indeed why
draw further attention to an attack on one's self? Nevertheless Pope, overriding the objection, with Steele and possibly
some others, concocted the devastating *jeu d'esprit* rather
lengthily entitled *The Narrative of Dr Robert Norris con-
cerning the strange and deplorable Frenzy of Mr John Denn–
An Officer of the Custom House* (a good deal more follows),
Dr Norris being a quack who advertised his ability to cure
lunatics. It is even now an extremely funny document, if
you let the more primitive side of your sense of humour
have play; it can hardly be called brutal – and if it were,
who was Dennis to complain? – because it is too fantastic to
be personal, and in a way too general. For what was really
struck at was not Dennis so much as the peculiar kind of
pedantry he stood for, and which Pope was to mock at till
the end of his days. It was much the sort of thing Swift did
when he tried to laugh the astrologer Partridge out of existence: in either case the writers hoped to kill something by

wild gusts of mirth. Broad farce? Well, yes. Here is a sample.
(We are at the point in the little play where the old woman
who 'does for' Dennis, believing him bewitched, has fetched
Dr Norris, who finds with the patient Lintot, to whose
interest it is, of course, for Dennis to be found perfectly
sane. The doctor is therefore told that Dennis's only ailment
is a swelling in the legs.)

DR	Pray, sir, how did you contract this swelling?
DENN	By a criticism.
DR	A criticism! That's a distemper I never heard of.
DENN	S'death, sir, a distemper! It is no distemper, but a noble art. I have sat fourteen days at it; and are you a doctor, and don't know there's a communication between the legs and the brain?
DR	What made you sit so many hours, sir?
DENN	Cato, sir.
DR	Sir, I speak of your distemper; what gave you this tumour?
DENN	Cato, Cato, Cato.
OLD WOM	For God's sake, Doctor, name not this evil spirit; it is the whole cause of his madness: alas! poor master is just falling into his fits.
MR LINTOT	Fits! Z— what fits! a man may well have swelling in his legs, that sits writing fourteen hours a day. He got this by the Remarks.
DR	The Remarks! what are those?
DENN	'Sdeath! have you never read my remarks? . . .
DR	. . . Pray, sir, of what are you sick?
DENN	Of every thing, of every thing. I am sick of the sentiments, of the diction, of the protasis, of the epitasis, and the catastrophe. – Alas! what is become of the drama, the drama?
OLD WOM	The dram, sir! Mr Lintot drank up all the gin just now; but I'll go fetch more presently.

The whole is sheer, high-spirited ragging, not very respect-
ful perhaps, but without malice or outrageous personalities;

for though Dennis comes out as an extraordinary oddity, he
is not unlikeable. What impelled Pope as much as anything
else was his possession, too often forgotten, of an enormous
sense of fun, especially as a young man. Addison, alas!
thought the entertaining squib most undignified, and caused
Steele on August 4th, 1713, to write an extremely odd note
to Lintot:

> Mr Lintot,—Mr Addison desired me to tell you that he wholly
> disapproves the manner of treating Mr Dennis in a little pamphlet
> by way of Dr Norris's account. When he thinks fit to take notice of
> Mr Dennis's objections to his writings, he will do it in a way Mr
> Dennis shall have no just reason to complain of. But when the
> papers mentioned were offered to be communicated to him, he
> said he could not, either in honour or conscience, be privy to such
> a treatment, and was sorry to hear of it. I am, sir, your very humble
> servant.

A little humiliating for Pope, since Steele must have told
him about it; an indirect but none the less galling snub;
indirect, for though Addison suspected Steele's share, he
probably did not know that Pope had a hand in the game.

IV

HOMERIC BATTLES

IN any event, how could Addison have been certain? In those days when so many figures big and little launched their work anonymously in the first instance (Addison himself, Swift, Steele, Defoe, Pope and nearly all their petty attackers), so as to see how the thing went, or what rows might occur, or indeed what prosecutions follow, before acknowledging it, it was an extremely tricky business to impute any given piece of writing to any one person. As for the *Frenzy* itself, Pope 'assured' Cromwell (who was perhaps glanced at in it) that he was not 'the' author, which he could after all do, if somewhat evasively, since he was only a collaborator, even if the principal one. Later on, by including it in his works he assumed major responsibility; but for the moment it remained merely one item in the bewildering conspiratorial goings-on of this and the next few years, part of the strange whirl of barely kept tempers and frayed or broken friendships, the bitter stress of party-mongering during an acute and prolonged crisis interweaving itself with literary incompatibilities. Dennis, not the least suspicious of mortals, soon came to think that Pope had been among those who induced Lintot to egg him on to write the *Remarks*, so that at one and the same time Addison might be stung, and Dennis lay himself open. It is unlikely. Naturally Pope may have thought that it would be only too good a stroke of luck if Dennis were to make himself out to the public to be a ponderous ass, but he was not yet in a mind to hurt Addison, or even to break with him at all.

But now Philips began to cause mischief. He was always polite to Pope, but from about now used to insinuate that he was caballing with Swift and other Tories to undermine the Buttonians, and destroy, not only Addison's reputation, but what was worse, his own. He was, in fact, Philips suggested, too Tory decently to frequent a Whig coffee-house; this in spite of the fact that the Tories were beginning to suspect Pope of Whiggery because he 'writ with Steele'. And indeed, though he abominated party – what had a man whose religion cut him out of all politics to do with party? – feeling ran so high that you had to owe allegiance to one side rather than to another; and Pope's affiliation would naturally be with the Tories, from whom Catholics might hope for more than they could possibly expect from the Whigs.

And as far as writing went, that is, in his moral being, Pope was far closer to Swift and Prior, Arbuthnot and Parnell, Tories all, than to any of the Buttonians. Together, with Harley, Lord Oxford, who would relax in their company after his labours as First Minister, they formed the 'Scriblerus Club', an anti-pomposity, anti-pedantry club, sworn to attack and defeat 'dullness', that is bad writing, in every form. Swift was now actively engaged in political pamphleteering on the Tory side, and could no longer hobnob with the others of his old triumvirate, Addison and Steele; his friends were the Tory Prior – an excellent poet – and Parnell, the Irish parson, one of the best among the minor poets of the time. Arbuthnot too, scientist, antiquary and doctor (he looked after Queen Anne), who was an admirable writer and the creator of John Bull. And there was Gay – though what the politics of that charming inconsequential person were Lord only knew; and above all the members, it was at this time Gay whom Pope most loved, Gay who helped him to pin-prick Dennis by mockingly dedicating his play of *The Mohocks* to him, and by later fleering Philips by making nonsense of his pastorals in his *Shepherd's Week*. What made these men different from any other group was their capacity for laughter – often real good Britanno-Rabelaisian laughter, and their indomitable sense of fun. Swift was notoriously mirthful; none, except possibly Parnell, was above ribaldry. Pope began the idea by suggesting in the *Spectator* of August 1712 that, as a balance to the monthly abstract *The History of the Works of the Learned*, he would issue every month *An Account of the Works of the Unlearned*, especially the English ones, 'who many of them make a very Eminent Figure in the Illiterate World'. It was not, however, till the spring of 1714 that the Club was actually formed, and it was decided to produce the work as *The Memoirs of Martinus Scriblerus*, which would spoof all pedantry and bad writing. But the collapse of the Tories in the summer, and the death of the Queen in August broke the Club up. Arbuthnot lost his post, Swift went to his exile in Ireland, where Parnell died in 1718. But the friendships formed produced lasting results, which we shall come upon.

But in any event Pope, in his general attitude towards life, was nearer the Churchmen than he was to the Dissenters, who were the main Whig support, for he believed less than Addison and his like did in science and progress and the Enlightenment generally, not to mention the Royal Exchange. Nevertheless he struggled to keep clear of the fray, as though to say 'What has poetry to do with politics!'

Yet, inevitably, he drifted into a sort of politico-literary gang warfare, though deploring it, and making fun of it where he could, as he did most brilliantly in another of his light-hearted spoofs. It is unlikely that anybody for long took seriously *The Key to the Rape of the Lock*, written early in 1715 by a mysterious Esdras Barnivelt, which made out with beautiful plausibility that the second version of the poem, published in March 1714, was of a 'dangerous tendency', obviously part of a dastardly Popish plot, that Belinda represented England, or the Queen, that the Lock stood for the Barrier Treaty and so on. Whether anyone was taken in would not matter, and on this occasion Pope made no attempt to hide his authorship. What did matter was that nobody in future should be so silly as to suppose that a political manifesto lurked behind every poem. For us it merely reveals Pope's ebullient gaiety and high spirits; and though, incidentally, it was not the sort of thing that Addison would find at all amusing, Swift would relish it enormously. It was partly a Scriblerian product.

Yet concurrently with all this a fiercer war was being waged in this year of 1715, in some ways the most eventful one in the whole of Pope's career, a twelve months of blasts and counterblasts, of manœuvrings and vilifications. The campaign had begun insidiously in the spring of 1714, and it makes a very queer story, the whole of which has only recently come to light: and however little one might wish to detract from Addison, it must be told if Pope is to be cleared of the imputation of undue and ungenerous malice.

In the autumn of 1713, the *Frenzy* affair having blown over, Pope, who saw no necessity for warring literary cliques, felt he was on good enough terms with Addison to tell him that he was thinking of embarking on a translation of Homer's *Iliad*, and asking his advice. Addison gave him

kindly encouragement, and by the end of the year the en-
gineering of the edition – by subscription – was in full
swing. Subscribers were coming forward well, and Swift
was especially active in bullying his acquaintance among the
great to put their names down for a copy – for several copies.
So on March 23rd, 1714, Pope was able to sign a contract
with Lintot, and all was set for a successful venture. The odd
thing was, that though subscriptions continued to come in,
Addison never procured a single one. He seemed less friendly
than he had been, and Pope began to be less conciliatory
towards the great man, who, it would seem, was coming to
feel a little guilty. At any rate at the end of August he spoke
to Jervas in a most kindly manner about Pope – in remarks
that were meant to be passed on. He had indeed, he confessed, been afraid that Swift had carried Pope 'too far
among the enemy, during the heat of the animosity' – that
is, in that tense crisis of spring and summer which had pre-
ceded the death of the Queen on the first of the month. But
now, especially as it had been rumoured that he was not too
eager that Pope should prosper as a poet – where did the
rumour come from? we may ask – he would do what he
could for him, the Whigs being royally back in power. Pope
was superbly cool. In his reply of the 27th, after referring to
'the scandalous meanness of that proceeding which was
used by Philips' to estrange him from Addison, he goes on
to say that much as he might wish for Addison's friendship,
he would expect nothing more than civility from him. At
the moment, alas! Addison was being misinformed by 'half-
witted creatures': but, he concluded, 'Mr Addison is sure of
my respect at all times, and of my real friendship, whenever
he shall think fit to know me for what I am.'

Civility – the word had then a more generous meaning
than it has now, and in the autumn Pope felt that he might

well make the courteous gesture to Addison of asking him
to look over the first book of his Homer, which he had so
readily advised him to translate. Addison's answer flabber-
gasted him. He was very sorry, the great man said, but his
young friend Tickell was also producing an *Iliad*, and he
had looked over the first book of that translation: to do the
same thing for Pope's would look like double dealing. But
any future books . . . well, delighted, charmed! A Tickell
Iliad! This was the first that Pope, or indeed anybody else,
had heard of it. Edward Young was as bewildered as Pope.
Why, he said, he and Tickell showed each other all their
verses, and this was the first whisper he had heard about an
Iliad. The truth was, as we now know, that on May 31st, a
little more than two months after Pope had signed his contract with Lintot, Tickell had signed another, not altogether
unlike it, with the rival publisher, Jacob Tonson. A very
curious affair. It was blazed abroad that Pope was doing a
Homer: Addison had encouraged him: yet here was Addison,
we are now certain, secretly encouraging Tickell! Anybody,
of course, has the right to publish a translation of anything
he wishes: but when the same great figure first encourages
a poet whom he knows to be a shaky classic, and then enters
into collusion with another who is a more than usually good
one, there is only one inference to be drawn: he wishes to
humiliate the former.

Pope was more than hurt: he was bitterly upset, because
success meant almost everything to him. If the edition went
well, he stood to make a very nice sum of money, a matter
of grave concern to him for several reasons, the immediate
one being that the French funds in which a little of his
father's capital was invested, were reducing their interest.
But there was a long term reason as well. Pope, constituted
as he was, needed a comfortable income if he was to lead the

kind of life essential to the development of his genius, and a
fiery pride made the idea of being dependent upon patron-
age abhorrent to him. He felt acutely that the position of
the author in his day was degrading, with its fulsomely
fawning dedications to great men in the hope of a large
banknote or a minor government post, with the alternative
of slavery to publishers, or selling one's self to the theatre or
to a party. Pope was determined to be free, to say what he
liked, and write what he wanted to, snapping his fingers at
persons or politics. As a matter of history, he was the first
Englishman living by his pen to be rid of humiliating
scheming: even though his concern may have been selfish,
he revolutionized the position of the writer in society; for as
it turned out he netted some £9,000 by his two Homers (say
£50,000 in our currency), and was set up for life. It was
something to boast of – and he often boasted of it, quite
legitimately. He was to say in 1737·

> But (thanks to Homer) since I live and thrive,
> Indebted to no prince or peer alive . . .

as in 1733 he had referred to himself as

> Unplac'd, unpension'd, no man's heir or slave . . .

and it was a magnificent achievement.

But in the autumn of 1714 none of this was at all certain.
Pope knew he was no scholar; his translation was being
accomplished with the generous help of earlier translators –
Dacier, Ogilby, Chapman: and though he had the advice of
Parnell, especially in the matter of learned notes, he could
not be sure that here and there he might not make a fool of
himself. Now that it was known there were rivals in the
field, each began to have his backers, and an odd tortoise-
race ensued, each trying to get the other to publish first, so

as to profit by his version. Pope's was originally announced for April 1715, but towards the end of the year before, Lintot stated that Pope had got on so fast that he would be ready with his copies in March. This, however, failed to bring out Tickell, and the waiting game went on, varied with sparring matches. For from now – they had indeed begun rather earlier – the lesser men, the Grub-Street fry, attacked Pope, occasionally spurred on by some private reason such as Dennis had supposed himself to have, but as far as we can tell usually unprovoked, unless instinctive antipathy may be called provocation. The attacks were partly political, partly literary gang-warfare, as appears to have been the case with Gildon, who as early as the summer of 1714 had produced a sharp enough satire on Pope, called *A new Rehearsal, or Bays the Younger.* Its chief job was to maltreat *The Rape of the Lock*, but it also scoffed at Pope's competence to translate Greek. Gildon – if this time it was he – returned to the attack early in 1715 with *Aesop at the Bear-Garden*, a flaunting comment on Pope's *Temple of Fame*, a Chaucerian adaptation he had put out in February. Most galling, perhaps, was the mock advertisement at the beginning of the volume, a humorous take-off of Pope's December announcement of his Homer, this one declaring that the first book of *Tom Thumb* would be 'transform'd from the original Nonsense into *Greek* Heroicks'.

It is likely that Pope was stimulated rather than distressed by a good deal of this, and he seems to have felt more confident about his Homer – or so he told Congreve. At all events, he on his side was having a little sport, he and Rowe helping Gay in that romping 'tragi-comical-pastoral-farce' aptly named *The What D'ye Call It*, a Scriblerus offshoot. This extremely amusing, still actable piece, makes fun of a good many things, including heroic tragedy; and, alas, the authors saw fit not to take as seriously as Addison wished his sublime presentation of Cato reading the Platonic essay on the immortality of the soul before committing suicide. They showed the almost illiterate hero of their play at the appropriate moment painfully spelling out the title page of *The Pilgrim's Progress*, 'eighth ed-it-i-on printed by Nicholas Boddington,' and at this point exclaiming 'Oh 'tis so moving, I can read no more.' Addison was always thrillingly sensitive to any suggestion that his play was not perfect, and just at this time he was especially touchy: for one thing he was not being rewarded for his political services as he thought he ought to be, and for another his comedy, *The Drummer*, had fallen dismally flat – though luckily nobody had the faintest idea that he was the author. So his friends went merrily to work on scarifying *The What D'ye Call It*, for which they produced a *Key*. In itself it was innocuous, but it was barbed by a Preface in which, as Gay put it to Caryll, the author 'with much judgement and learning calls me a blockhead and Mr Pope a knave', referring as it did to

> the baseness of a busy Pen, which is now attacking all the Reputations which rais'd its own, and screens itself behind a borrow'd name . . . this *malevolent Critick* fights . . . behind the shield of *impenetrable Stupidity*.

Two charges in one – cowardice and treacherous ingratitude.

Pope did not answer; why should he? the laughers would be on his side. But within a day or two something much more threatening appeared in the form of a booklet entitled *Homerides*, written, anonymously, by Thomas Burnet (the youngest son of the famous Whig Bishop), and George Duckett. Addison knew about it, and made the authors cut out the degrading remarks about Pope's person which were part of the controversial armoury of those days, perhaps even altered the original title, *The Hump Conference*, though a sufficiently stinging Greek motto was left in. Burnet told Duckett that Addison had taken out the defamatory remarks not from love of either him or Pope, but merely to make the pamphlet more effective. There were two versions – or indeed numbers – the second appearing towards the end of May; they both attack Pope for his outrageous presumption in daring to tackle Homer, and rollick sarcastically about Pope's greed for money.

But still nobody's *Iliad* appeared, and the extraordinary game in which each tried to play cat to the other's mouse went on. At last, tired of waiting, Pope announced that he would issue his four Books on June 6th: Tickell's was at once advertised, and came out on the 8th, two days after Pope's.

A tense, breath-holding moment for Pope. It was true that his rival in his Preface declared that:

> ... when I begun this First Book, I had some thoughts of translating the whole *Iliad*, but had the pleasure of being diverted from that Design, by finding the Work was fallen into a much abler Hand:

and that this one Book was only a specimen to solicit subscriptions for the *Odyssey*, in which he had 'already made some progress'. Nobody, however, was taken in by this piece of nursery innocence, which within a month was viciously as well as devastatingly parodied, perhaps by Pope or one of his adherents. But already it did not matter, for in the interval the critical battle had been decisively fought in Pope's favour, his adversary, as he put it, having sunk before him without a blow. There were, to be sure, strictures on his version, but even Oxford preferred it, in spite of Tickell's having been Professor of Poetry there. Pope's *Homer* was

popular: it was readable, it went with a swing, it was
dramatic, rapid, and in brilliant verse. It is true that the
great scholar Bentley (so it is reported) said 'It's a very
pretty poem, Mr Pope, but you mustn't call it Homer'; but
the criticism, however well founded it may be, was irrele-
vant; for what Pope had laboured to produce, and success-
fully, was a good English poem. He did indeed absorb some
of Tickell's happier strokes in his later edition; but then
Pope was always ready to acknowledge himself in the
wrong – where it was a question of art.

The matter, one would think, might have been left to lie
there; but the Buttonians and other buzz-flies (such as were
later to refer to Pope as 'the little Wasp of Twickenham')
kept up intermittent sallies as might have ruffled a saint.
Pope, to the glory of letters, was no saint, and he was infuri-
ated – against Addison in the main. The Little Senate, it
seemed, had been told to take the line that Tickell's was the
best translation ever published: both versions, of course,
were good, but Tickell's had more Homer in it. The worst
side of Pope's suspicious nature was aroused. He did not yet
think that Addison had done Tickell's version for him –
Steele was to tell him that in the Preface to *The Drummer*
published after Addison's death – but surely the latter must
be behind the barbs by way of paragraphs or advertisement
which appeared sporadically in the press. Ingratitude, dis-
honesty, incompetence, spite, greed, those were the qualities attributed to Pope, while jeers at his physical deformity
provided an accompaniment which to-day we would not
consider amusing. There seems to have been only one
favourable Grub-Street document – but then came Addison's review in *Freeholder* 40, of May 7th, 1716 – almost
too suave and courteous. Had he been pulled up sharp?

It is possible that he had received the early draft of his

'character', which still, as that of Atticus, sings out from the
vibrant pages of the *Prologue to the Satires*. It is certain that
at about this time 'the malice and juggle at Button's' as
Lintot called it, little by little begot in Pope the scathing
paragraph, first of all as a sentence or two in a letter to his
friend Craggs, the brilliant young politician, who was to be
prematurely cut off by the smallpox – such phrases as 'We
are each of us so civil and obliging, that neither thinks he is
obliged': then, not much later, in the autumn of 1715, the
first rough draft began to take shape, scribbled on the backs
of letters from his friends, as was the custom with 'paper-
sparing Pope' as Swift called him. There, for instance, we
read the couplet:

> But our Great Turk in wit must reign alone
>   no living near
> & ill can bear a Brother on ye throne

which became the swinging:

> Should such a man, too fond to rule alone,
> Bear, like the *Turk*, no brother near the throne . . .

Then, as the lines, devastating because so nearly true,
approached perfection, he sent them to Addison. 'He used
me very civilly ever after', Pope was to tell Spence some
twenty years later, 'and never did me any injustice that I
know of, from that time to his death, which was about three
years after.' As Addison died in the middle of June 1719, it
would seem that Pope did not withhold his satire very long,
with the gratifying result that he was praised in the *Freeholder*.

Yet if, as is usually said, Addison's phrase about Tickell's
version having moreof Homer in it than Pope's was the final
provocation, it would be a very small one for sending any-

thing so fiercely biting, even though it were written.
Actually, Lord Warwick, Addison's stepson, told Pope a
story, which he believed, that the great man was paying
Gildon to libel him in 'a thing about Wycherley'. What the
'thing' was remains in some doubt owing to a certain con-
fusion of dates, and it may have been Gildon's *New
Rehearsal*, of April 1714, as some think, or *The True
Character of Mr Pope*, suspected of being by Gildon and
Dennis. But it was more probably the *Memoirs of Wycherley*, a Grub-Street biography of Pope's ancient friend which
contained a viciously malevolent attack on Pope, of which
a few samples will do by way of illustration:

> About this time there came to Town, and to *Will's*, one *Pope*,
> a little diminutive Creature, who had got a sort of Knack in smooth
> Versification and with it was for setting up for a Wit and a Poet . . .
> . . . Plausible, or at least Cringing Way of Insinuation . . .
> . . . this little *Aesopic* sort of an animal in his own cropt Hair, and
> Dress agreeable to the Forest he came from . . . (Aesop being a
> cripple)

and worst of all the paragraph ended with an insulting
reference to Pope's father, who had recently died. Well, of
course, that was not Addison's way – he was a far bigger
man than that – but such things would work up a man like
Pope to a blind berserk rage when he resembled, as his
enemies suggested, the Thersites he so admirably described
in Book II of the *Iliad*:

> Awed by no shame, by no respect controll'd,
> In scandal busy, in reproaches bold:
> With witty malice studious to defame,
> Scorn all his joy, and laughter all his aim:

It seems more likely that it was then that he sent the lines,
especially as the phrase 'Gildon's venal quill' originally

occurred there. The dates don't fit in very well, but it is easy to get confused about time when thinking of events of twenty years ago, and Pope was less accurate than most of us in that respect. The date does not really matter, except that to choose the later one makes the beautifully directed virulence of the satire more comprehensible.

The lines do not seem to have been freely passed about until after Addison died, though Lady Mary Wortley Montagu among others saw them; but before long they were piratically printed from time to time, first in the *St James's Journal* of December 15th, 1722; Pope owned them publicly by printing them in the *Miscellany* he published with Swift in 1727. Intermediately, however, he had sent to Tickell the adulatory *Epistle to Addison* to be placed in the forefront of the *Works* Addison's disciple was editing in 1721; and later, in the *Epistle to Augustus* gave him full due – in some respects. Pope could be generous: if he was only too acutely aware of Addison's very grave faults, he could also give him credit for his shining virtues: but the virtues, we notice, belong to the writer, the crimes to the man; the matter for tears being that they were both housed in the same body.

But, of course, in about 1716 Pope was at the highest pitch of nervous irritability, though not yet at the summit of his nervous vigour. He had still to establish his position firmly, and he was in the thick of the fray, a little diminutive hero desperately battling against ogres. He was living a very full life, straining every nerve – in writing poetry, and in translating Homer, about which he used to have nightmares: 'I dreamed often of being engaged in a long journey, and that I should never get to the end of it,' he told Spence. And above all this he was enjoying the social life of a writer among men of letters and in the delightful aristo-literary

society of the day. The wonder is that he should usually be
so good tempered. In all that time, continually provoked,
goaded, meanly lashed by foes lurking in ambush, he only
struck back twice with any bitterness. The strokes of his
enemies are forgotten, his are remembered – they were so
infernally effective. If nothing else had, the Atticus portrait
would have made Addison immortal; and if the steps taken
with Curll hardly by themselves make for that printer's
survival, they were notoriously drastic.

Edmund Curll – 'odious in his person, scandalous in his
Fame', as Defoe described him, had intermittently cut at
Pope, latterly becoming his principal tormentor: he had
taken the lead in the Pope-baiting that succeeded the publication of the first volume of Homer. The attacks were all
according to pattern – gibes at Pope for being a despicable
scholar, a liar, a cheat, an ingrate, an indecent writer (a
thrust that came near home), a dangerous friend – and dis-
gustingly deformed. Pope might have let Curll and his
minions pass by unnoticed – but that the publisher did an
unforgivable thing. Through, it appears, a poor historian
called Oldmixon, who filched them for him, he got hold of
some slightly scandalous satirical 'Town Eclogues' mainly by
Lady Mary Wortley Montagu, at that time much Pope's
friend, and published them under the title of *Court Poems*.
Explaining that he had found them in a pocket-book someone had dropped, he went on to say that the best opinions
had ascribed them to Lady Mary or to Gay (who had indeed
probably written one), but that Addison had said they could
only be by 'the judicious translator of Homer'.

This amusing, and beautifully plausible 'advertisement',
made Lady Mary furious, and she and Pope between them
grew so hotly enraged, that two days after the publication a
very odd incident took place. Lintot asked Curll to discuss

some publishing matter with him at a tavern, and after a while Pope came in, upbraided Curll for having published the *Court Poems*, listened to his explanation, seemed appeased, and offered him a glass of wine. Curll accepted, Pope poured him out the wine from a bottle which was not the one his own glass was filled from. After a while Mr Curll felt uncomfortable, and soon desperately ill – the vomitory being effective and cruelly disagreeable. Then Pope went home and gleefully wrote a pamphlet called *A Full and True Account of Horrid and Barbarous Revenge by Poison on the Body of Mr Edmund Curll* – a ruthless, jeering performance, but here and there not without wit. To us the episode seems unbelievable: but the age accepted it quite placidly, for after all Pope could not thrash the man, the normal procedure of those days, nor toss him in a blanket as the scholars of Westminster shortly afterwards did. Even Congreve, the most gentle, urbane, 'unreproachful' person, could some years later write to Pope suggesting that Curll was ripe for another emetic. And after all, was Pope's action half so brutal as the things Curll was doing to him? Moreover, Curll was not long in gaining satisfaction in a way he could not be struck back at for. A little earlier, Pope, to amuse his tavern companions had written a parody, not so much of the first Psalm, as of Sternhold's metrical version; this was something he was quite entitled to do, but it must be admitted that Pope's parody is ribald. Curll got hold of it, and published it, whereupon Pope, unable to ignore the attribution, put into the press two notices in which he used a phrase which might be taken to mean that he knew nothing of the poem, but might equally well, and actually did mean, that he knew nothing of how it had come to be published. It was cleverly done he thought; and writing to Teresa Blount on August 7th, 1716, he remarked:

'If you have seen a late advertisement, you will know that I have not told a lie (which we both abominate), but equivocated pretty genteelly . . . ' Pretty genteel equivocation served the turn as well as might be, as it was to do again often enough in Pope's life.

And at about this time there took place another broil, it can hardly be called less, this time with Cibber, the playwright and actor-manager, who had been one of Pope's early, ill-judged tavern acquaintances, as was to appear years later. It arose out of a frolicsome enough play called *Three Hours after Marriage*, put forward under Gay's name, but actually almost as much by Pope and Arbuthnot – in fact a Scriblerian production. It gibed at all sorts of things, especially at one of Arbuthnot's rivals, Dr Woodward, satirized as Fossile, a quack: Dennis was there as Sir Tremendous the critic, and even Cibber was taken off as an actor-manager, in lines he himself uttered. Cibber from the first hated the play, and did his best to make it fail; and though it was running well, partly because of certain light-hearted obscenities which were found delightful even by Court ladies, a little maliciously replaced it with Buckingham's *Rehearsal*. According to tradition he brought it up to date, this time by having an amusing gag about *Three Hours*. This made Pope white with rage, quite unjustifiably. He is supposed to have gone to Cibber in a trembling fury, told him he was a rascal, and that he would cane him if he could, but that Gay was a properer fellow to do it. The next night then, Gay burst in, berated Cibber in the same way, and got a fillip on the nose; all of which raised such an uproar that the Guards had to part them, and carry Gay off.

And then in the midst of all this bother came, inevitable as doom, Dennis's attack on Homer. He chastised it with his familiar whips and scorpions. Pope's version was absurd, extravagant, full of solecisms and barbarous English, in short a fearsome travesty. But Pope had an answer ready up his sleeve, namely Parnell's version of *The Battle of the Frogs and Mice*, with a Life of Zoilus prefixed, in which Pope's methods were more than plausibly defended. Following this satisfaction, Pope was able to have a little quiet fun with Cibber's play, *The Non-juror*, which, in a supposed 'letter' to Rowe named *The Plot Discover'd*, he made the play out to be an anti-Government Jacobite libel.

Too much space, it may be thought, has been given to this scrabbling and clapper-clawing aspect of Pope's life: but it is necessary to have a clear view of this phase, for almost the whole of his days were passed in this atmosphere of vitriolic attack, as often as not directed by sheer personal malice against him. Yet underneath this frothy discoloured surface the main current of Pope's almost serene genius flowed steadily and gravely, a genius for friendship as well as for poetry. Without a little dwelling upon this formative – or if you like deformative – phase, it would be difficult to understand Pope's later work, to sense behind it the whole contrast between his outer life of controversy and anger, and the inner life of quietude, to see how it came about that all the while superb mellifluous poetry gave a sheen and a dazzle to the utmost sordor, making even the *cloaca* honourable and vituperation lovely.

V

SETTLING DOWN

But what, it will be asked, had Pope up to now done to justify the place he holds in the world of letters? How far had he gone along the road to becoming the 'correct' poet dedicated to perfection? And here we may look at the contents of the first volume of poems consisting wholly of his *Works*, beautifully produced by Lintot in 1717. There are to be found the poems already mentioned, and besides other pieces, many of them minor, two completely new ventures, *Eloisa to Abelard*, and the *Elegy to the Memory of an Unfortunate Lady*. The earlier poems were here and there revised a little, since Pope rarely left a poem alone to the very end of his life. If no student of Pope's poetry would wish to neglect a line of his writing, the brief biographer must content himself with inviting his readers to whet their appetite with snatches at these last-named works and *The Rape of the Lock*, which was now presented in its final form.

The completed *Rape of the Lock* is a jewel of many facets, each shining brilliantly. It is, in the first place, a mock-heroic poem, in those days a form very much delighted in; so when readers were met at the outset with:

> What dire Offence from am'rous Causes springs,
> What mighty Contests rise from trivial things,

they knew exactly where they were, and when the theme
was announced:

> Say, what strange Motive, Goddess! cou'd compel
> A well-bred *Lord* t'assault a gentle *Belle*?
> Oh say what stranger Cause, yet unexplor'd,
> Cou'd make a gentle *Belle* reject a *Lord*?

they could settle down to an enjoyment they understood.
The great increase in the size of the poem was the result of
Pope's deciding to introduce the 'machinery' of the classical
epic; but instead of gods, he took the sylphs he had discovered in an esoteric cabbalistic work, *Le Comte de
Gabalis*, by the Abbé de Villars, and in doing so he contrived
an enchanting iridescence: for these creatures with insect-
wings were:

> Transparent forms, too fine for mortal Sight
> Their fluid bodies half-dissolv'd in Light.
> Loose to the Wind their airy Garments flew,
> Thin glitt'ring Textures of the filmy Dew;
> Dipt in the richest Tincture of the Skies,
> Where Light disports in ever-mingling Dyes,
> While ev'ry Beam new transient Colours flings,
> Colours that change whene'er they wave their Wings.

Yet this shimmering background served not only as a
delight in itself, but as a setting for good hard-hitting wit,
social criticism, and a real philosophy subtly indicated by
giving a sense of the fullness and richness of existence combined with a moral sense which put everything in its proper
proportion. The wit was not only the obvious satire of the
famous:

> The hungry Judges soon the Sentence sign,
> And Wretches hang that Jury-men may Dine;

but more delicate things, such as putting together in one
line the puffs, powders, patches, bibles, *billets-doux* of

Belinda's dressing-table, or the asking whether the black
omens of the day portended that:

> ... the Nymph shall break *Diana's* Law,
> Or some frail *China* Jar receive a Flaw,
> Or stain her Honour, or her new Brocade,
> Forget her Pray'rs, or miss a Masquerade,
> Or lose her Heart, or Necklace, at a Ball;
> Or whether Heav'n has doomed that *Shock* must fall ...

The whole apparently artless document, moreover, was
phrased in such dulcet terms, with such lovely music, that
you could very well miss the point. But, you might well ask,
what point? because there were so many in this very complex affair. It could appeal to the scholar from its magnificent and learned fooling of the classics – the descent into
Hell being converted into the drop into the Cave of Spleen
(though Pope was not the first to think of this), the Games,
the Battle, the ascent into Heaven; all that was beautifully
done. And besides, there was now introduced in this final
form, by way of a glorious passage 'imitating' Homer, the
application of poetic ideas to life, voicing the hunger for the
perfect existence, which is, alas! conditioned by the moral
law:

> Oh! if to dance all Night, and dress all Day,
> Charm'd the Small-pox, or chas'd old Age away;
> Who would not scorn what Huswife's Cares produce,
> Or who would learn one earthly Thing of Use?

the whole being linked with previous poets, classical as well
as English, by an amazing wealth of allusion, of clever
echoes and adaptations, of parodying and punning, not as a
mosaic, but as something organic and flowing, and in its own
right lovely, that with its exquisite music was quite enchanting. In the conclusion all immediate concerns, all social

adjustments, all morals, all satire, disappear in a splendid rocket-shower of pure poetry, which yet seems all the time to have direct connexions with what we feel about life:

> Then cease, bright Nymph! to mourn thy ravish'd Hair
> Which adds new Glory to the shining Sphere!
> Not all the Tresses that fair Head can boast
> Shall draw such Envy as the Lock you lost.
> For, after all the Murders of your Eye,
> When, after Millions slain, your self shall die;
> When those fair Suns shall set, as set they must,
> And all those Tresses shall be laid in Dust;
> *This Lock*, the Muse shall consecrate to Fame,
> And mid'st the Stars inscribe *Belinda's* name.

You can take the poem as simply as you like; but, if you like, you can find it full of complexities, and of values which go far outside its ostensible meaning.

And if in going to the heroical epistle (another recognized 'kind') Pope retained his seductive music, it was a different sort of music, involving another set of images, of words, of allusions, which will delight the real taster of literature: but at the same time Pope was deeply conscious of the main object of poetry, which is to move the general reader in matters based on universal passions. He found his subject in the still fresh story of Eloisa and Abelard, a version of whose letters had lately been published in England. Those who feel that passion cannot be expressed in the couplet find it meaningless, and schoolgirls are said to adjudge it cold and artificial: but Byron, who knew something about the emotions, asked in connexion with this poem, 'If you search for passion, where is it to be found stronger?' And you feel as you read the poem that Pope is almost sobbing as he follows the movements of Eloisa's heart, her attempted denial of her love in favour of her religion, her temporary

conquests of herself, her helpless returns upon herself. The
theme is expressed fairly soon, in all the 'romantic' setting
of a gloomy landscape:

> Ye rugged rocks! which holy knees have worn;
> Ye grots and caverns shagg'd with horrid thorn!
> Shrines where their vigils pale-ey'd virgins keep,
> And pitying saints, whose statues learn to weep!
> Tho' cold like you, unmov'd, and silent grown,
> I have not yet forgot myself to stone.
> All is not Heaven's while *Abelard* has part
> Still rebel nature holds out half my heart . . .

and what holds the reader throughout – if he has an ear – is
the muted loveliness of the phrasing, the changes in tempo
and in vowel sound to follow the varying moods of Eloisa,
all making an impressive setting for the terrible emotional
struggle set before us, the hankering for the 'Eternal sun-
shine of the spotless mind' in the shining portrait of the
vestal virgin, swinging away to 'Far other raptures, of
unholy joy'. The success of the poem (it is either a moving
success for you or an utter failure, there is no half-way) is
the result of the complete fusion of the story told and the
means to tell it. You cannot distinguish at any moment
whether you are affected by the story or by the words with
all their movement and their overtones.

And as what might be called a pendant to this piece, Pope
brought out the equally romantic *Elegy*. The identity of the
lady does not matter, since the whole thing is excessively
vague: all you know is that the young woman was wronged
by her family, and died abroad:

> By foreign hands thy dying eyes were clos'd,
> By foreign hands thy decent limbs compos'd,
> By foreign hands thy humble grave adorn'd,
> By strangers honour'd, and by strangers mourn'd!

That change of tune is followed by a change of rhythm, which sets other nerves going, to pass through a little scornful satire to a lovely lilt, giving yet another tune to express Pope's passion for the country, the paragraph going on to end with a little formal 'poetization':

> What tho' no friends in sable weeds appear,
> Grieve for an hour, perhaps, then mourn a year,
> And bear about the mockery of woe
> To midnight dances, and the public show?
> What tho' no weeping Loves thy ashes grace,
> Nor polish'd marble emulate thy face?
> What tho' no sacred earth allow thee room,
> Nor hallow'd dirge be mutter'd o'er thy tomb?
> Yet shall thy grave with rising flow'rs be drest,
> And the green turf lie lightly on thy breast:
> There shall the morn her earliest tears bestow,
> There the first roses of the year shall blow;
> While Angels with their silver wings o'ershade
> The ground, now sacred by thy reliques made.

Pope now, we see, had complete mastery over his medium; the sustained passage, the modulations within it, the subtle variations of sound and speed and emphasis at different points of the line. Though elements of that kind of verse and imagery and sentiment were to enter into his later poetry, never again was Pope to write a poem wholly in that manner.

For some years indeed he was to write hardly any poetry at all, except for his translation of Homer, that steady thirty to fifty lines a day. And indeed he was gathering himself for new things, extending his circle of real friends, and changing his mode of life. It was in 1715, in his 'Farewell to London', that he,

> The gayest valetudinaire,
> Most thinking rake alive,

had written, since 'Homer, damn him! calls':

> Luxurious lobster nights, farewell,
>   For sober, studious days;
> And Burlington's delicious meal,
>   For salads, tarts, and pease.

But he was not for long to be buried so far away in the country, and was to come nearer to London than in the days of his early literary adventures. In 1716 the family, as Catholics threatened with land tax, sold the little estate at Binfield, and came to Chiswick, near Lord Burlington, so influential a man in the development of English taste in houses and gardens, and already, as we see, one of Pope's friends: but in October of the next year, Pope's father died, and in the autumn of 1718 he moved with his mother to the house he rented at Twickenham.

It was a pleasant dwelling, suitable for housing his mother, whom he was devotedly to cherish till her death some fifteen years later. It was roomy enough to entertain modestly in, to hold a guest, and to provide a study for refuge. A little lawn in front of the house ran down to the river, which so often flooded the grass plat that nothing much could be grown around it. But behind the house was a garden of about five acres which was a source of infinite pleasure to Pope, and is important in the history of English taste, because Pope was very much in the forefront of the new movement in gardens which broke away from the rigid geometrical pattern fashionable in the 17th century. For his school the straight line was abhorrent to nature, and therefore should not occur in gardens. Pope did not go the whole hog in this, but he hated to see nature hacked about and bullied, 'trees cut to statues' in fact: and as early as 1713, in *Guardian* 173, he had stated his preference for 'simple nature's hand, diffusing artless beauties o'er the place'. Yet there had to be some formality at Twickenham, for there was everything, a large mount and two small ones, a double grove, a bowling green, a vineyard, an orangery, a kitchen garden, connected up where connexion was necessary by straight or winding alleys, giving interesting glimpses of the river, with the sails passing across as in a telescope. Later on, at the far end, Pope erected an obelisk to his mother. The whole was very complete, a little landscape in miniature, 'three inches of gardening' as he called it affectionately, with that love of the miniature he shared with Swift. Yet after all it was not so tiny: you can do a good deal with five acres, even though you do call it 'a bit of ground that would have been but a plate of sallet to Nebuchadnezzar, the first day he was turned to graze'.

Unluckily the house backed on to the road from Hampton Court to London, and thus was separated from the garden by a highway. So Pope got a passage dug from the front of the house, under the pleasant terrace where you might sit out, to the garden behind; you emerged facing the small temple, at the end of the 'wilderness' walk. 'Pope's excavation was requisite as an entrance to his garden,' Dr Johnson was to remark, 'and, as some men try to be proud of their defects, he extracted an ornament from an inconvenience, and vanity produced a grotto where necessity enforced a passage'. Well, there may have been a touch of vanity at the beginning, but the celebrated grotto was a delirious fantasy in which Pope let himself go; for year after year it was his great toy, his unfailing release, and he kept on improving and enlarging it, lining the walls with different kinds of stone and crystals, ores and corals, arranging mirrors to enhance the effect, placing a thin alabaster lamp to strengthen the glooms, and contriving the most cunning waterworks, little cascades and rills, which twisting about made gurgles and splashes, and a 'little dripping murmur'. In the summer it was deliciously cool, and you could sit and talk in it, at any rate in theory. It was all in the tradition – from classical times to the Renaissance – and Pope had spied out grottoes in Windsor Forest when writing his poem. Others were to imitate his work and ask his advice, as they did also in constructing their gardens; in fact, with such famous professionals as Bridgeman and Kent, he became a recognized authority, and left his mark on many great estates.

That is the setting in which one should imagine him, working outwards as though from the centre of a web – and indeed in one of his early squibs, *The Club of Little Men*, when making brave fun of his littleness, he described himself as 'a lively little Creature, with long Arms and Legs: A Spider is no ill Emblem of him': from this centre he could feel everything that was going on either at great country houses, or in Grub-Street, sensitive to it all:

> The spider's touch, how exquisitely fine;
> Feels at each thread, and lives along the line.

But also the creature dashes out to get its nutriment, or its prey. And Pope, of course, was always busily harvesting material for his poetry, or brooding over the ills done him and his art, making the ills themselves matter for his poetry. For, devoted son and tireless friend though he was, he knew that only through 'obstinacy and inveterate resolution' could a man write poetry, for 'it is such a task as scarce leaves a man time to be a good neighbour, a useful friend, nay to plant a tree, much less to save his soul.' For Pope, the salvation of his soul would follow upon his writing the best verse he could, and the other things he did indeed find an amazing amount of time for. But he would never rest: far more than with Shaftesbury, the fiery spirit forcing out its way, fretted the pigmy body to decay. 'Descend, in the name of God,' Swift implored him, 'to some other amusements [than writing poetry], as common mortals do. Learn to play at cards, or tables, or bowls; get talking females ... ' but these things he never did, except a little get talking females, such as 'Patty' Blount (but she was a devotion), Lady Suffolk with other Court ladies, and once at least the aged but still redoubtable Duchess of Marlborough. No cards, or tables or bowls: but there was, after all, the grotto.

It should have been peaceful enough, but there was always something happening to Pope to agitate him, to set his nerves tingling; and at the beginning of the twenties he was to suffer agonies of anxiety, on account, first of a work of literary piety, secondly of an honoured friendship. Both troubles hinged upon accusations of Jacobitism, a good stick to beat Catholics with. He had laid himself all the more open to the attack since in 1721 he had written an 'Epistle to Lord Oxford' at the forefront of the edition of the *Poems* of Parnell, who had died in 1718. The Epistle, a fine and dignified poem, was a courageous tribute to a friend in disgrace, not altogether unattended with danger; it was beautifully generous, for however evasive Pope might be (almost as it were by instinct), when it was a question of honouring or helping a friend he would volunteer anything. No legal action could be taken about the 'Epistle to Robert, Earl of Oxford and Earl Mortimer'; but when in January 1723 Pope produced an edition of the *Works* of the Duke of Buckingham (John Sheffield, who as Lord Mulgrave had written the then famous verse *Essay on Poetry*), the kind of person who sniffs out that sort of thing sniffed out a Jacobite tendency in one or two of the poems. It was probably Curll, who with Gildon and others was concerned with an unauthorized edition of the Duke's poems, which the Lords (on the ground of breach of privilege) had severely lopped, at the same time killing a prefatory 'Life' by Lewis Theobald. Although Pope had returned Buckingham's verse compliments in kind, yet it was with some reluctance, and largely because Atterbury, Bishop of Rochester, added his pleas to those of the Duchess, that he undertook to edit the works. Seeing that a well-known printer, Alderman Barber, had got the original permission to publish the peer's writings, Pope had not bothered much to comb through them for possible anti-governmental implications, and was profoundly shocked when three days after the handsome volumes had appeared, they were officially seized. Pope saw that he might be held responsible for the supposed 'reflections . . . cast upon the late happy Revolution', and was concerned for his own safety; in the previous August his friend Atterbury had been thrown into the Tower. There was 'a cry upon him' in the Press: he was accused of having got a patent to print by showing only some of the material, keeping the seditious stuff up his sleeve. One paper, representing him as writing to the shade of the Duke, 'I am obliged *to keep no Faith with Hereticks;* in which article of my Religion (as much as I have ridiculed most others) I have constantly been very punctual', suggested that he had outraged obligations here as much as he was assumed to have done with regard to Addison and Steele. The whole thing was nerve-racking, especially as his intimacy with Atterbury was known: and indeed he was called upon to give evidence as to the Bishop's blamelessness at his trial for treasonable correspondence with the Pretender. We now know him to have been guilty, but at that time proof was not forthcoming. Pope may have known something, but also he may have been used as a screen. At any rate there was not much he was going to say at the trial, except that Atterbury had never spoken treason in his presence: they had discussed literature and the technique of verse. But although he knew most of the peers on the front bench, he stammered and bungled such evidence as he had to give.

And, alas! all this came at a most unfortunate moment, just when he was about to float his scheme for a translation of the *Odyssey*. However, by the autumn of 1723, Atterbury was safely exiled, and the Buckingham affair had blown over, the *Works* being in circulation: so Pope could once more go on with the arrangements for Homer. It would have been impossible to do this while the flurry was on, since this was to be not only a subscription business (and he felt he needed money since extra taxes were imposed on Catholics in 1723), but also a collaborative affair with an Anglican parson, Broome, and a non-juror Fenton, scholars and poets in their own right. While he was under suspicion it would have been most inadvisable to take any steps at all. This, however, could now go forward, and Pope busied himself with it. Not that he had in the meantime been idle, for before Atterbury's arrest he had begun his edition of Shakespeare – the second of the five in the first half of the century to help to satisfy that age' scraving for the works of the greatest of English poets. As Tonson was to reap the benefit, and he himself was simply to be paid a sum down, the issue did not depend on his political respectability; so Tonson could get on with soliciting bountiful subscriptions, and Pope could get on with the work. He collected a large number of early texts, proceeded to get what advice he could from his friends, and settled down to what he called 'the dull duties of an editor'. No good Scriblerian would wish to be too self-important about a bit of what was, after all, merely useful pedantry: the pity was it did not strike him that if you consider work dull, you are not likely to do it well.

As for the *Odyssey*, the business side of the affair offered some nice little problems. Pope wanted to go on with Homer, there was money in it; but then he didn't want to do too much work on it, and so obtained his two helpers. But how much ought the public to know about this? After all, it was Pope's work they would buy, not Broome's or Fenton's. The secret, however, leaked out, because Broome could not keep his mouth shut, and it had to be impressed on him that it was to his advantage to conceal exactly what his part was. The advertisement concocted to lure subscribers was very evasive: the translation was to be, not 'By the translator of the Iliad', but 'undertaken by him', – a pretty piece of genteel equivocation. Then there were 'Proposals by Mr Pope, For a Translation of Homer's Odyssey,' not 'Proposals for a translation by Mr Pope.' The difficulty really was that the collaborators were torn between the desire for money and the vanity of glory. Lintot, who had been persuaded to do the job – Tonson hanging back – also helped to bungle matters (he became 'that fool,' or 'such a fool' in the correspondence) and had continually to be watched for mean tricks. The situation became strained: Broome and Fenton were afraid that Pope would get the lion's share (as of course he did, and quite rightly), and they would get no praise. 'Be assured,' Broome wrote to Fenton, 'Mr Pope will . . . I fear not give us our due share of honour. He is a Caesar in poetry, and will bear no equal.' It was a trying time Pope had, what with versifying his own share (at the same time as editing Shakespeare and looking after a sick mother), urging his helpers to get on with their work, and keeping them from blabbing too much. At the conclusion of it all, however, Pope somehow induced Broome to add a fulsomely adulatory poem at the end of the *Odyssey*, and a postscript in which he stated he had done three books, and Fenton two, out of the twenty-four. It was only confessed some years later, very quietly, almost tacitly, that Broome had actually done eight books, and Fenton four, though Pope slipped into the apparatus of the 1729 *Dunciad* that he himself had done only twelve. He did, however, oversee the rest. Fenton died in 1730, and never showed any bitterness; Pope helped him in 1729 with his splendid edition of Waller. There was, however, for some years a little sparring between Pope and Broome, but after Pope had shown his teeth a little in two or three publications, in 1735 matters were ostensibly patched up.

Shakespeare was published in March 1725, the first three volumes of the *Odyssey* in April. Much the same things were said about the new Homer as had been said about the old: Pope knew no Greek, could not translate, should not have used rhyme, and at any rate it was all monstrous journey-work done with the help of hireling scribblers. Pope was probably used to this by now: the great thing was that people read and enjoyed his popularization, and what is more, bought it: he netted about five thousand pounds. The work also brought him the friendship of a charming young scholar, Joseph Spence, whose criticisms were so modestly phrased that Pope demanded to make his acquaintance. But the reactions to his Shakespeare were another matter; they got under his skin. In spite of his protestations that he was a 'preserving' editor, he had made a number of capricious emendations, revealing all sorts of ignorance; and though he was in many ways a pioneer, with some idea of what the problem was later to turn out to be, and did indeed produce here and there an emendation accepted by future editors, the work was in the main an amateurish bungled sort of affair. He had worked with paid and unpaid assistants, and a number of dabblers. So now Theobald got to work. He had earlier been friends with Pope, but had not unnaturally taken hard the suppression of his Life of the Duke of Buckingham, and, though he had for some years written a good deal about Shakespeare, had not responded to Pope's public appeals for help. He may claim to rank as our first real Shakespearean scholar. Pope's superficiality outraged him (just as incompetence in poetry outraged Pope), and in March 1726 he published *Shakespeare Restored: or, a Specimen of the Many Errors . . . Committed . . . by Mr Pope*. The attack is not on Pope either as a person or as a poet; Theobald really did want to see a decent text of Shakespeare. He was by no means himself the impeccable editor, and he is sometimes absurdly pedantic: but if many of his emendations have been rejected by his successors many have lasted; Pope in his second edition of 1728 accepted a good few of his corrections and restorations. But Theobald's attack – different from the usual Grub-Street malevolence – ruined Pope's reputation as an editor: the show-down rankled, and the gall was to give rise to surprising results.

VI

FRIEND AND SATIRIST

F ROM the picture just drawn it might seem that Pope was
in process of sinking deeper and deeper into the mire of
quarrels and vituperations: but at just about this time there
emerged the mature Pope, a man in a definite and definable
way different in being from the earlier Pope, the Pope on
his way to his real greatness. A change happens to most
writers as they grow older; they cease to dance, and walk
only for a purpose, and Pope at this time seems to have
undergone some kind of climacteric. It is common to ascribe
the change in the kind of poetry Pope wrote to his new
friendship with Bolingbroke, who returned from exile in
1725, and came to live not far from him at Dawley; but it
may well seem that Bolingbroke, far from influencing Pope
so much as has been supposed, was, rather, the whetstone
upon which Pope sharpened his new attitude. It might be
more revealing to date the change from Swift's visit to him
in 1726 with *Gulliver's Travels* in his pocket. It may be even
that it was *Gulliver's Travels* which brought about the
change in Pope, for there is no book so calculated to make a
man examine the very roots of his being. In a way, of
course, *The Dunciad* of 1728 flows directly from this new
commerce with the old co-member of the Scriblerus Club,

and is a curious half-way house between the old Pope and the new – a farewell on the one hand, departure to a new adventure on the other. And to have been with Swift at Twickenham in those crucial days must in itself have been a terrific experience, perhaps not so much because of what Swift said, but of what he did not say, and of how he looked. Swift's deep 'pessimism' in the philosophic sense, his disbelief in the perfectibility of man, his acceptance of evil, must have had a profound effect upon Pope, who, in spite of his Catholic upbringing, tended rather to the optimism Lord Shaftesbury had helped to popularize, and which he found echoed, if modified, in Bolingbroke.

Thus Bolingbroke and Swift, experience, and indeed age, brought about the change in Pope, to which we must add the deepening of his friendships. Naturally, in looking at Pope's life as a casual spectator, you are apt to see only the constantly recurring crises and dramatic moments, to hear the clash and the cries. Pope was ever, it is true, all over the place, a great traveller within the bounds of England, constantly visiting friends, chiefly at great houses where he would get comfort, the opportunity to model gardens, and feel that he was with people who mattered; and if anything was likely to happen in London, he would dash up – often by boat – to get the excitement of it. And with his sick sensibility he was always anxiously alert to hear or read what was being said about him; he collected, and had specially bound up, in four volumes, all the attacks, justified or scurrilous, which were made against him. If he liked to be at the centre of the great worlds of thought or action, he could not leave alone the world of Grub-Street, had to be the spider quivering at the centre of his web, dashing out on forays. For the Pope who is obviously visible, social life was a kind of perilous game, in which one fought for advantage, unscrupulously, mendaciously if need be, always showing one's self at one's best, concealing one's meannesses. Was not the life of a wit one warfare upon earth?

But there was another Pope, the thoughtful poet and the devoted friend. The older he grew, and the more enemies he aroused to fury, the more he came to ponder life, and the more deeply to value friendship. The theme occurs again and again in his letters, in such a way as to attest the genuineness of Pope's feeling: the phrases ring true. There is no need for him to have been posturing before Gay (as he did before many people) when he wrote in October 1730 what Gay could so easily have seen through if it had been a lie:

> Nature, temper, and habit from my youth made me have but one strong desire. All other ambitions, my person, education, constitution, religion etc. conspired to remove far from me. That desire was, to fix and preserve a few lasting dependable friendships . . .

and to Swift in 1736 (March 25th):

> I am a man of desperate fortunes, that is, a man whose friends are dead: for I never aimed at any other fortune than friends . . .

and these were to be found among men of his own kind, that is, writers with something to say. To these must be added Martha Blount, with whom for years he passed a good deal of his time nearly every day, and whose attendance on him grew in the end so constant as to be a little tiresome to some of his friends, invidious to his acquaintance. At one time certainly he had been in love with her, so frenziedly anxious about her when she had a chill as to accuse her mother and sister of wanting to kill her because they insisted on a minimum of fresh air and floor-scrubbing. His enemies have accused him of making her his mistress, a charge his friends have hotly refuted, though some to-day for his sake might wish it had been true. At all events, whatever the relation, her sympathetic blue eyes, famous even when she was old, were always a succour and a comfort to him.

But except in such moments of relaxation as calmer hours with his friends might give him, Pope was always indefatigably busy with poetry, never without some poetical scheme in his head, as Swift put it. He simply had to write, and be always garnering material, jotting lines or phrases or paragraphs down on the nearest scrap of paper, the back of a letter or an envelope, re-hashing or revising. In his next phase of writing, when he was often at work on more than one poem at a time, lines or paragraphs would be shifted from one to another. The idea, the observation, the person, the emotion, seems to have forced itself into full consciousness (slid in a verse, or hitched into a rhyme) first, perhaps, in a phrase or a couplet. But his unit was chiefly the paragraph; and such units he would polish, fit into place somewhere, alter, change with relation to the poem or poems, every time becoming more perfect, more expressive, bettered for sound or sense, and either more pointed or more general as he needed. This process went remorselessly on, even at night, for he was a bad sleeper, and writing materials were kept at his hand: then fools rushed into his head, and so he wrote.

And since now that, in 1726, with Homer and Shakespeare off his hands – except for consequential squabbles – Pope was free to enter new fields, it was just the right moment for Swift to re-appear. His first occupation after his reunion in March with Scriblerian and other friends not seen for twelve years, was to devise the anonymous publication of *Gulliver's Travels*, in which Pope helped him, by arranging to have the MS. mysteriously dropped at the

6

publisher's house 'in the dark from a hackney coach', after
he had gone back to Ireland: there were some parts it might
not be wise to own at the moment. His next task was to put
together with Pope a mass of old stuff, the *Miscellanies*,
partly Scriblerian; and indeed, the next three or four years
were to be a kind of revival of the Club, a triumphant
festival: *Gulliver* itself was partly Scriblerian, some of the
first voyage, and a good deal of the fun with scientists of the
third having probably at least been sketched out in 1714
with Arbuthnot: then in 1728 Gay produced *The Beggar's
Opera*, the 'Newgate pastoral' that Swift, as a Scriblerian,
had asked for in 1716; and finally, in the same year, *The
Dunciad*, in fact three pieces of enduring literature in as
many years.

It was while Pope and Swift were discussing their old
work at Twitnam (to use the then familiar pronunciation),
that *The Dunciad* was begotten. Pope had by him some
scribbles of satirical verse, that odd scrap or two on the back
of some bill, and after reading them over, was about to
throw them into the fire. But Swift saved them, and suggested that many such should be strung into some sort of
poem, so as to wound, excoriate, and if possible utterly
demolish and metagrobolise the dunces. He afterwards
claimed half credit for the birth, which Pope willingly
granted him: but the period of gestation was, naturally,
long. In the meantime the two prepared their *Miscellanies*,
Volumes I and II appearing in June 1727. Swift was back
again that year, to see through the 'last' volume (it was
not the last, since the 'third' appeared in 1732), which
should have contained the poem – up till then known as
Dulness – that he had urged Pope to write. But to his dis-
appointment, when the volume did appear, instead of this
poem he found an old Scriblerian piece called *The Bathos*

(Peri Bathous) or *The Art of Sinking in Poetry*, to which he and all the others – Gay, Arbuthnot and Parnell, had contributed morsels of fatuous absurdity from other poets, chiefly Pope's critics. There is plenty of fun in it, and plenty to infuriate the victims: it is also good criticism: but it was not the poem Swift had hoped for.

Pope had changed his mind. For one thing his new poem was not ready; it was becoming too big for the *Miscellanies;* and besides, there would be advantages in publishing this first, as a *ballon d'essai*, or, as has been suggested, a kind of ground bait to produce more folly. Grub-Street stirred uneasily. It was rumoured – he had been careful to let the secret out – that Pope was about to publish 'A Burlesque Heroick on Writers', and on May 11th a letter (which Pope ascribed to Dennis) appeared in a paper to say that Pope would publish a poem called 'The Progress of Dulness'–the dullness, the writer suggested, having begun with *Windsor Forest*! Luckily however, Pope had foreseen the danger of the name, and what appeared on May 18th was *The Dunciad*. The method of publication was odd. The work was anonymous, said to be reprinted from a Dublin edition, and a good deal of mystery attached to it. There was nothing to connect it with Pope or Swift, since the promised dedication to the latter was missing. The idea was conveyed that this was a pirated edition, and Pope got his publisher to file a bill in chancery to have the sale restrained; but in any event such an edition would, of course, force the author, whoever he might be, to bring out a perfected one. In the meantime he would be able to see whether he might be moved against for libel. Everybody, of course, knew it was Pope's, and on the day of its sale a whole posse of minor authors and Grub-Street paper-men mobbed the bookshop, entreating, and threatening law, or battery, and crying treason to try to prevent the sale of a book the hawkers were clamouring to get – according to Savage, who was to help Pope in the next edition by collecting literary gossip for him. It is possible that he ran some danger from violence, and it is certain he was threatened. But he did not let this affect him. As his halfsister Mrs Rackett told Spence,

> My brother does not seem to know what fear is. When some of the people that he had put into his Dunciad, were so much enraged against him, and threatened him so highly he loved to walk out alone. . . . Only he would take Bounce [his enormous Danish bitch] with him; and for some time carried pistols in his pocket.

Pope told Spence that he would not go a step out of his way to avoid attack: 'he thought it better to die, than to live in fear of such rascals.' He was far more afraid of possible libel actions, so before his 'correct' publication came out, he transferred the copyright to three of his friends in the peerage, Lords Oxford, Burlington and Bathurst, whom no scribbler would dare attack. It was soon found safe enough for them to pass it on to a regular publisher.

Even in those days, in London itself, the poem was largely incomprehensible without notes, as Swift complained, though he praised the poem highly. But, as Pope reassured him, a proper edition was coming out 'attended with *Proeme, Prolegomena, Testimonia, Scriptorum, Index Authorum* and *Notes Variorum*', all the immense apparatus being part of the fun, the Testimonies, Prolegomena and many of the notes being by no less a person than Martinus Scriblerus himself. To anyone in the know, this mock heroic poem, or, as it has been called, this 'ludicrous, grotesque, lifesize shadow cast by a piece of an epic poem,' to anyone with a slight knowledge of the epic form, and a considerable knowledge of contemporary literature, the work is a glorious and immensely funny work, filled much more with rollicking good humour than with bitterness, and a work of consummate art. To the modern reader, unprepared to take the trouble to understand it, even the *Dunciad Variorum* of 1729 will be largely blank; yet there are things in it which will attract either by their beauty, their grotesque impropriety or the sheer obvious nonsense. It has layer upon layer of implication. In, for example, the lines where Pope is describing Lintot running in the race:

> As when a dab-chick waddles thro' the copse,
> On feet and wings, and flies, and wades, and hops . . .

you are expected to realize several things: first that it is an exquisite piece of nature description, based on accurate observation: secondly how ludicrous Lintot would look running in that way; thirdly that this is a parody of the 'games' episode in a classical epic; and fourthly that it is a reminder of the lines in *Paradise Lost* where Milton describes Satan as he, skirting the abyss,

> With head, hands, wings, or feet, pursues his way,
> And swims, or sinks, or wades, or creeps, or flies.

Or you can just enjoy it as a melodious couplet. There are here and there lines and passages of moving lyric grace, and his own favourite

> Lo! where Mæotis sleeps, and hardly flows
> The freezing Tanais in a Waste of Snows.

The victims, of course, did not enjoy any of it, and there were various retorts, a famous one being *Pope Alexander's Supremacy and Infallibility Examin'd* – probably by Dennis and Duckett – the frontispiece to which pictured Pope's head on a body of a particularly nasty monkey, the text describing him as 'an misshapen Hump of Malice and Ill-nature'. But then what did Pope really believe he was doing in this poem? He was in part, of course, scoring off his old enemies and critics, and especially was he trying to destroy Theobald, 'piddling Tibbald', whom he made the King of the Dunces. But that would not be enough to make Swift proud of the invocation:

> O thou! whatever Title please thine ear,
> Dean, Drapier, Bickerstaff, or Gulliver!
> Whether thou choose Cervantes' serious air,
> Or laugh and shake in Rab'lais' easy Chair . . .

and so on. He liked, naturally, to be associated with Pope, but only in something of real worth. And what was attempted in this poem was a cleansing of the domain of letters. Both men were sensitively aware of what they believed to be a catastrophic decline in standards: Grub-Street was posturing as 'Literature' with a capital L, the drama was in rapid decay. And since to both bad writing was a crime, not only a painful laceration but something corrupting (as it is), an insidious evil like the death-watch beetle in beams of a cathedral, they would do their best to laugh it out of serious consideration. It was *The Bathos* in a completer, more sweeping form. There is little that is bitingly vindictive, nothing of the cruel treatment to which Pope was continually subject: it is indeed enormously good-humoured, even tolerantly so, for how should superior beings get angry with children? It is often asked, why need he have wasted time over such minimal creatures? Part of the justification is that he has made them so – in his day they were, many of them the big figures – quite rightly apart from Bentley and Defoe, in whom, certainly, Pope made a grave mistake. But then Defoe undoubtedly did write shocking poetry, and Bentley was an old story from Swift's early days with *The Battle of the Books*.

In any event, it was a turning point in Pope's career, and in it he was able to work off a great deal of his ire: but it was more important than that, since it marked a new phase. He was putting behind him more obviously imaginative work, what he called 'wandering in Fancy's maze', and was 'stooping to Truth to moralize his song'. He, of course, did not quite see the implications of what he was setting out to do – it was to become clear in two or three years – but on looking back he must have realized that he had always to some extent moralized his song. Satire had early been a small element in his work, especially, of course, in *The Rape of the Lock*; he had long before 'versified', though not yet printed, two of Donne's satires (Parnell had done a third): and Atterbury ('mitred Rochester') after seeing the first draft of the Addison portrait had told him that satire was his bent.

Yet the whole business of *The Dunciad* seems to have wearied him a little, especially as there was one distressing circumstance connected with the poem, namely the final departure of Swift. If the visit of 1726 had been gloriously successful, from Pope's point of view, though clouded for Swift by the illness of Stella which he then thought fatal, that of 1727 had a melancholy conclusion. Pope's mother was ailing, Pope himself was not very well, and the 'little nightingale' voice, always light, could not penetrate the ears of Swift, who was suffering all that summer from his deafness and giddiness. The two friends had to sit silently together, Swift miserable, seeing his final political hopes decline with the unexpected return to power of Walpole after the death of George I, and Stella giving renewed anxiety. He went away to London, saying he would come back to Twickenham, but left for Ireland without seeing Pope. He did, however, write him a letter, which, unfor-

tunately, we have not got, though we have Pope's acknowledgement, and Swift's reply. There can scarcely be anything
more moving in the whole of intimate literary history, than
the letters these two great men, and great friends, ex-
changed on that occasion.

Pope to Swift. Oct. 2nd, 1727.

It is a perfect trouble to me to write to you, and your kind letter
left for me at Mr Gay's affected me so much, that it made me like
a girl. I cannot tell what to say to you; I only feel that I wish you
well in every circumstance of life; that it is almost as good to be
hated as to be loved, considering the pain it is to minds of any
tender turn, to find themselves so utterly impotent to do any
good, or give any ease to those who deserve them most from us.
I would very fain know, as soon as you recover your complaints,
or any part of them. Would to God I could ease any of them, or
had been able even to have alleviated any! I found I was not, and
truly it grieved me. I was sorry to find you could think yourself
easier in any house than mine, though at the same time I can
allow for a tenderness in your way of thinking, even when it
seemed to want that tenderness. I cannot explain my meaning;
perhaps you know it. . . .

Swift to Pope. Dublin, Oct. 12th, 1727.

I have been long reasoning with myself upon the condition I am
in, and in conclusion have thought it best to return to what for-
tune has made my home; I have there a large house, and servants
and conveniences about me. I may be worse than I am, and I have
nowhere to retire. I therefore thought it best to return to Ireland,
rather than go to any distant place in England. Here is my main-
tenance, and here my convenience. If it pleases God to restore me
to my health, I shall readily make a third journey; if not we must
part as all human creatures have parted. You are the best and
kindest friend in the world, and I know nobody alive or dead to
whom I am so much obliged; and if ever you made me angry, it
was for your too much care about me. I have often wished that
God Almighty would be so easy to the weakness of mankind as to

let old friends be acquainted in another state; and if I were to write an Utopia for heaven, that would be one of my schemes. This wildness you must allow for, because I am giddy and deaf.

And although he goes on to say how well Pope could be accommodated at the Deanery, the effect of the letter was like a door banged for ever.

And so, once the stimulus of all the excitement of *The Dunciad* was over – it had 'knock'd down' *The Beggar's Opera*, as the latter in conformity with Swift's hopes had 'knock'd down' *Gulliver* – a profound lassitude, a sense of fatigue and futility, overtook him. He wrote to Gay early in October 1730:

> ... I am sunk into an idleness, which makes me neither care nor labour to be noticed by the rest of mankind. I propose no rewards to myself, and why should I take any sort of pains? Here I sit and sleep, and probably here I shall sleep till I sleep for ever, like the old man of Verona.

And to Caryll in December:

> As to your question if I am writing, I very rarely dip my pen. The vanity is over: and unless I could hope to do it with some good end, or to a better pitch than I have hitherto done, I would never return to the lists. But the truth is, it is now in my hopes, God knows whether it may ever prove in my power, to contribute to some honest and moral purposes in writing on human life and manners, not exclusive of religious regards [not altogether just for Caryll, that] and I have many fragments which I am beginning to put together. ...

The vanity is over! Not quite, as the next sentence shows; something is already in the wind, and the person who had pulled him out of his despondency, and given him a fruitful idea, was the amateur farmer at Dawley.

VII

THE PHILOSOPHER

HENRY ST JOHN, Viscount Bolingbroke, has for more than two centuries had what we might now call, in our jargon, 'a bad press'. As a statesman he made a mistake, his philosophy went out of fashion, and Macaulay detested his politics. But lately he has been coming a little more into his own; philosophers are beginning to relent and take him seriously, and political thinkers treat him with respect. To both Swift and Pope, he seemed far above anybody they knew for sheer intellect and brilliance. Although Swift never loved him as he had loved Harley, he was from the first dazzled by him, thought his the best all-round mind he had ever met, while Pope regarded him almost as a demi-god. That should be enough commendation for most of us. He and Pope had not known each other much in the Queen Anne days, and it took a little time for them to get closely acquainted after Bolingbroke's return from exile: but soon Pope was exchanging visits, and going to Dawley Farm, and it was there that he began seriously to consider philosophy. We find Bolingbroke writing to Bathurst in October 1730:

... I expect to see Pope to-morrow, for my servant says he is at home, in which case I shall dine with him. You will not be forgot by us, for though we are deep in metaphysics, there will be some

gay scenes interspersed, which will of course lead us to your
lordship . . .

in short Pope was already 'deep' in the *Essay on Man.*

He had, indeed, been at it some time, as part of the
grandiose 'poetical scheme' which was to fill the rest of his
life; and Spence, now playing the part of a devoted Boswell,
has kept a record of conversations during his stay with him
for a week at the beginning of May 1730. The scheme was
(or at least by 1733 had become so) to produce two books of
'Ethic Epistles', the first one of which, 'Of the Nature and
State of Man,' known to us as the *Essay on Man*, was
actually completed; the second, 'Of the Use of Things',
arrived only at the stage of the *Moral Essays* we possess, and
passages in a final *Dunciad*. Matters were always taking new
shape in Pope's mind – as happens when the creative
imagination is at work – and the first sample of this great
venture was the 'Epistle to Lord Burlington' *On Taste*,
which afterwards became the fourth Moral Essay, the second
one 'On the Use of Riches'. It was mainly on taste in country
houses and their surroundings, and at one time Pope used to
refer to it as 'the gardening poem'. These *Moral Essays*,
even though they have plenty of humour, and here and
there some lovely passages, probably seem to the modern
reader the dullest of all the things Pope wrote; the morals
are unwaveringly trite. What appeals to him most are the
satirical 'characters' of which each Essay contains at least
one; the 'Essay on Woman' has three. But that was where
the trouble began, for there was an immediate outcry
against Pope for his portrait of Timon in the Epistle to Burlington, supposed (probably wrongly) to be the Duke of
Chandos, who had been kind to Pope. Pope stopped to consider, and in the next year there appeared only the 'third'
Pope-Swift *Miscellany* (mostly Swift), though all the while

Pope was, by way of keeping up his spirits, carrying on a clandestine war with the Dunces in the *Grub-Street Journal*, an ironical Scriblerus-like periodical he had much to do with, and in which he employed to help him what his enemies called his 'scavengers'. The next Epistle then – the one to Lord Bathurst 'On the Use of Riches' (Moral Essay No. 3) – did not appear until January 1733, but on its heels there came something far more exciting, the first 'Imitation of Horace'.

It was here that Pope found his most personal medium of expression, and produced in some ways his loveliest and certainly his liveliest work. It was partly accidental. In the previous year he had been very ill, prostrated by grief for the death of his beloved Gay,

> Of manner gentle, of affections mild;
> In wit, a man! simplicity, a child:

as he wrote in the epitaph which Dr Johnson might find a bad poem but which breathes affection. While he was in bed Bolingbroke came to see him, and found him reading Horace's *Satires;* picking up the volume he turned to the first satire of the second book, and in view of the vituperation Pope was then enduring on account of the Timon portrait, suggested that it fitted his case very well, and that he might English it for his amusement. Pope seized on the idea, translated it, he told Spence, in a morning or two, and after a fortnight or so sent it to the press as a defence against the attacks he felt sure would follow his Epistle to Bathurst, which fear of fuss had made him keep back some time. It was an admirable choice, for it contains a conversation about satire and the position of the satirist. How far the idea was altogether Bolingbroke's it is hard to say: it may have been Swift's example which set off Pope, for Swift had attempted that very satire, and in the old Queen Anne days had translated and published others.

At all events, one of the great virtues of these satires and epistles was their being partly autobiographical, and they enabled Pope to carry out a long – and most entertaining – campaign of self-justification. It is permitted to think that these Horatian 'Imitations' are the best, certainly the most characteristic things he ever did. The whole man pulsates in them – his intense nervous responses to nature and to man, his exquisite sensibility and lovely feeling for the music of the word and phrase, his generosity, his implacable enmity, his humour, his hatred, his warm friendship, and his deeply stirred patriotism. The form, colloquial, easy, so adapted for frequent variations in tone, was the happiest thing he could have discovered. The amazing thing is that though often the translation is so close, it nearly always reads like an original. The 'imitations' form a considerable amount of his work in the next ten years – they interfered sadly with the great didactic structure he was erecting – and posterity being duly thankful that they did, we may look at them all now. Though it has been finely said of these poems that when he is most in chains he seems most to dance, it is arguable that the greatest of them all are those 'imitations' based on no particular poem of Horace's; they are nevertheless what Horace might have written had he been Pope in the fourth decade of the eighteenth century. It is those perhaps we may consider here, though nobody would wish to miss the 'Epistle to Augustus' nor the charming lyrical Ode translated as a compliment to his young friend 'silver-tongued Murray', who afterwards became Lord Mansfield, the famous Lord Chief Justice.

The most glorious of all is the 'Epistle to Arbuthnot' – afterwards put into dialogue form and known as 'The Pro-

logue to the Satires', which he addressed to his old friend
when, in 1735, he was dying. It is at once an apologia for his
own life, and an affectionate tribute to the old Scriblerian,
who had also doctored him. One passage illustrates both
these aspects:

> Why did I write? what sin to me unknown
> Dipt me in Ink, my Parents', or my own?
> As yet a Child, nor yet a Fool to Fame,
> I lisp'd in Numbers, for the Numbers came.
> I left no Calling for this idle trade,
> No Duty broke, no Father dis-obey'd.
> The Muse but serv'd to ease some Friend, not Wife,
> To help me thro' this long Disease, my Life,
> To second, ARBUTHNOT! thy Art and Care,
> And teach, the Being you preserv'd, to bear . . .

the next paragraph going on to further self-justification.
And the really fascinating quality of this piece, which dis-
tinguishes it from most of the others, is the change in movement which gives it an almost dramatic quality, and the
variations in mood which lead him from affectionate remin-
iscence to the most virulent attacks he ever made. And this
is perhaps the place to insist that what he attacked was
always the mean, the life-denying thing, anything restric-
tive of the full flow of nature, of which the *Essay on Man* is
largely a hymn of praise. This is also, perhaps, the place to
insist that he was hardly ever, if at all, the aggressor in the
viciously wordy wars: his victims had always offended in
some way or other, which they, and ordinary coarse mortals,
might not have thought very wounding, but which hurt
Pope poignantly. The matter is to the point here, because
in the *Prologue* comes that masterpiece of searing, shrivell-
ing satire, the character of *Sporus*, Lord Hervey.

Hervey was probably led into gibing (rash man!) at Pope

by Lady Mary Wortley Montagu, who had become estranged from her vivid little neighbour at Twickenham in
about 1725, nobody quite knows why, possibly because he
had made her a declaration of love which she had met with
a fit of immoderate laughter, a cruelty she was quite capable
of, perhaps because she had returned unwashed some sheets
he had lent her, so deeply offending his mother. Pope pursued her nearly all his life with deft little bayonet jabs in
most of his satires; while some couplets, which might have
been of general scandalous application, she was ill-advised
enough publicly to take to herself. She became great friends
with Hervey, a niminy-piminy official at Court, all airs and
graces and intrigue, a sort of neuter, but very intelligent –
his *Memoirs* are extremely amusing as well as being an
invaluable source for historians. The crown of his offence
was to compose with Lady Mary *Verses addressed to the
Imitator of Horace*, wherein Pope was told he was dull and
that

> – none thy crabbed numbers can endure,
> Hard as thy heart, and as thy birth obscure;

three observations any one of which would make Pope livid
with fury. Hervey's mind, moreover, was neutral, unformative, uncreative, just the sort of negative thing Pope
loathed; and this loathing he expressed with an icy disdain
which proves his complete artistic control of his now perfected medium. It is worth looking at, though it ought to
be read aloud:

POPE	Let *Sporus* tremble.
ARBUTHNOT	What? That thing of silk,
	Sporus, that mere white Curd of Ass's milk?
	Satire or Sense alas! can *Sporus* feel?
	Who breaks a Butterfly upon a Wheel?
POPE	Yet let me flap this Bug with gilded wings,

This painted Child of Dirt that stinks and stings;
Whose buzz the Witty and the Fair annoys,
Yet Wit ne'er tastes, and Beauty ne'er enjoys:
So well-bred Spaniels civilly delight
In mumbling of the Game they dare not bite.
Eternal Smiles his Emptiness betray,
As shallow streams run dimpling all the way.
Whether in florid Impotence he speaks,
Or, as the Prompter breathes, the Puppet squeaks;
Or at the Ear of *Eve*, familiar Toad,
Half Froth, half Venom, spits himself abroad,
In Puns or Politicks, or Tales, or Lies,
In Spite, or Smut, or Rhymes, or Blasphemies;
His Wit all see-saw between *that* and *this*,
Now high, now low, now Master up, now Miss,
And he himself one vile Antithesis.
Amphibious Thing! that acting either Part,
The trifling Head, or the corrupted Heart!
Fop at the Toilet, Flatt'rer at the Board,
Now trips a Lady, and now struts a Lord.
Eve's Tempter thus the Rabbins have exprest,
A Cherub's face, a Reptile all the rest;
Beauty that shocks you, Parts that none will trust,
Wit that can creep, and Pride that licks the dust.

If that seems harsh, Hervey had deserved it, as he had merited the devastating prose *Letter to a Noble Lord* Pope had composed – a withering exposure. Pope did not publish it, since Walpole asked him not to, and though Pope had no love for the First Minister, the latter had begged an Abbey for Pope's old friend Southcote from the French Minister Fleury. The *Letter*, luckily, exists; but for the moment 'Sporus' did well enough to lash Hervey: moreover the name was general: the satire need be applied only by those who knew; and it was those who counted.

How Pope was able to 'work' the 'Epistle to Arbuthnot', fit in the mosaic pieces so that the transitions are perfectly

smooth, is almost miraculous. The poem has a delightful
rhythmic structure, great verbal beauty, with touches of
deep feeling which are really moving. As in all the poems
where he is autobiographical he does no doubt protest too
much about the perfection of his own character, but that is
permissible. Only a fool washes his own dirty linen in public.
But as time went on, something else crept in to his verse,
namely his political concern; for he had come, through
Bolingbroke, to frequent the company of the group of able
and highly placed young politicians who were in opposition
to Walpole. They were known as *the Patriots* (all oppositions
claim that title; it is always the government that plays party
politics), and they inveighed against the corruption of the
time, inveighed so well, and with such powerful pens, including Pope's, that posterity has ever since believed them.
As a matter of truth the times were no more decadent and
corrupt than they had been; in fact they were if anything
less corrupt, for thanks to the new system of Cabinet government everything had to be much more public and above-
board. At all events, Pope, imbued perhaps with Swift's
pessimism, surrounded with disappointed politicians, faced
with the decline of writing, as he thought, very much 'went
in with' the Boys, as Walpole called his young opponents.
They were certainly an interesting and honourable group,
cultivated, charming, who really did care for the welfare of
their country (so of course did Walpole; but it was his peace-
at-any-price policy they abhorred), and who, for the most
part, had lovely country houses which they liked 'improving'. There were, besides Bolingbroke, their leader till he
retired disgusted to France in 1735, Lyttelton, Marchmont,
and, rather older, Chesterfield and Pulteney, not to mention
the very much liked model of virtue, Lord Scarborough,
who committed suicide. Chief of all, perhaps, was Lord

Cobham, who created the house and grounds at Stowe, of which Pope wrote to a friend, 'If anything under Paradise could set me beyond earthly cogitations, Stowe might do it'. There the patriots used often to meet, to be joined before very long by a young cavalry subaltern called William Pitt. Pope very much relished all this society, and became more and more involved in politics. He flung on his shoulders a fine cloak of Roman republican virtue, adorned with a foolish little frill of king-hating. He felt he was at the centre where things are done – always a temptation to a man of letters, especially for one who, like Pope, because he was a Catholic, has all his life been excluded from any kind of action. For us, the important thing is that it gave his satire a nobler butt.

It is with this in mind that must be read the last great 'Imitation', the two 'Dialogues, Something like Horace' called originally *One Thousand Seven Hundred and Thirty Eight*, afterwards the *Epilogue to the Satires*. This is Pope at his best in this kind, and you feel his greatness as a man as well as a poet. Both Dialogues, the second especially, move along with perfect ease, covering a deal of ground, in verse varying from the happily colloquial (the last triumph of a verse writer) to the prophetic strain, and back again to the friendly and warm. This marvellous symphonic mastery can be shown in a very short space, by quoting a passage or two which follow close upon one of the grittiest in the whole of his canon, a nauseating simile about Westphalian hogs, not at all in the taste of to-day. Soon his interlocutor, a little goaded by Pope's rather high manner (a considerable streak of humour runs through all this), irritated perhaps by the preposterous claim:

> Ask you what Provocation I have had?
> The strong Antipathy of Good to Bad . . .

(the always virtuous Mr Pope!) ventures to say, 'You're
strangely proud'. This allows Pope to make a splendid statement about himself which at the same time indicts the
whole administration, then to lay, so to speak, the sword of
his pen upon the altar of the Muse he had chosen as his
goddess, and finally to swing into four lines of the sheerest
lyrical loveliness.

> Yes, I am proud; I must be proud to see
> Men not afraid of God, afraid of me:
> Safe from the Bar, the Pulpit, and the Throne,
> Yet touch'd and sham'd by *Ridicule* alone.
>   O sacred Weapon! left for Truth's defence,
> Sole Dread of Folly, Vice, and Insolence!
> To all but Heav'n-directed hands deny'd,
> The Muse may give thee, but the Gods must guide.
> Rev'rent I touch thee! but with honest zeal;
> To rouse the Watchmen of the Public Weal,
> To Virtue's Work provoke the tardy Hall,
> And goad the Prelate slumb'ring in his Stall.
>   Ye tinsel Insects! whom a Court maintains,
> That counts your Beauties only by your Stains,
> Spin all your Cobwebs o'er the Eye of Day!
> The Muse's wing shall brush you all away . . .

That breath-taking last statement, superb as it is, persists
like a little Mozartian tune that you hum as you go about
your daily avocations.

So much for the Horatian work, by which perhaps Pope
lives most for us: but he himself, and most of his contemporaries, would have ranked him highest for his *Essay on
Man*, the first part of which appeared in February 1733, two
more coming out before the end of May, the fourth and
final part being delayed until January 1734, Pope's mother
having died in June 1733, to his great grief and temporary
exhaustion. It is an amazing performance, anonymous till

published as a whole, which has been dubbed muddled and even inchoate, but which to anyone at all familiar with the field of thought Pope was covering, is a masterpiece of organization. It sums up, in an extraordinarily small space, what might be called the popular philosophy of the day, that is, the assumptions underlying the behaviour and beliefs – even the religious beliefs – of the vast mass of educated men, a 'philosophy' based largely on the now obsolete ideas of the Chain of Being (replaced by Evolution), and the doctrine of Plenitude – that is, of every chink of Nature (spelt with a capital N) being filled up, no conceivable form of life being left out. That much from medieval ideas going back to Plato. To this was added the new idea of the immensity of the Universe that Newton had revealed, with its staggering mechanism; and all the infinitude of tiny life the newly-discovered microscope had shown to man. It was a popularization of contemporary feeling and up-to-date knowledge, and through it ran a good deal of Stoic moralizing about man's pride; it also involved an attempt to solve the problem of evil – to vindicate the ways of God to Man. It sounds monstrous, but it happens also to be, very often, poetry, of the kind that is still read, that is still relevant to our present situation. So much so, that when Mr Churchill made a speech at Harvard in 1949 he quoted (not quite complete) the opening of the second Epistle:

> Know then thyself, presume not God to scan,
> The proper study of mankind is man.
> Placed on this isthmus of a middle state,
> A being darkly wise, and rudely great:
> With too much knowledge for the sceptic side,
> With too much weakness for the Stoic's pride,
> He hangs between; in doubt to act or rest;
> In doubt to deem himself a god or beast

In doubt his mind or body to prefer;
Born but to die, and reasoning but to err;
Alike in ignorance, his reason such,
Whether he thinks too little, or too much:
Chaos of Thought and Passion, all confus'd;
Still by himself abused or disabused;
Created half to rise, and half to fall,
Great lord of all things, yet a prey to all;
Sole judge of truth, in endless error hurled:
The glory, jest, and riddle of the world.

as glorious a piece of 'philosophic' poetry as ever was penned.

It is sometimes said that all that Pope did was to versify Bolingbroke's prose; that is nonsense. Bolingbroke did indeed often jot down notes of their conversations, and further, wrote rather considerable rough essays; and sometimes Pope used these scripts. Again, it is almost universally stated that Pope got all his philosophy from Bolingbroke. But why? Pope had always read philosophy, from those early days when he had browsed in his father's library at Binfield: he was steeped in contemporary work, and knew his Locke and Ray, his Shaftesbury and Leibnitz, as well as his Montaigne and Pascal. He had no doubt read Archbishop King's work on the origin of evil, which written in Latin in 1704 had been translated into English in the twenties. It seems common sense to suppose that Pope and Bolingbroke had read the same books and discussed them; but why suppose further that the argument was all with Bolingbroke? After all, Pope had a brain; and in actual fact, in some respects his philosophy as given in the poem differs from Bolingbroke's in the latter's *Works*. Moreover a considerable number of the ideas in the *Essay* may be found in some of Pope's earliest letters, long before he knew Bolingbroke, at any rate years before he became 'deep in metaphysics' with him. But Bolingbroke, to be sure, did suggest the poem, and helped Pope to arrange it; Pope submitted his plan to him, discussed a hundred details, and in the splendid lyrical passage which ends the poem makes full acknowledgement to his 'guide, philosopher and friend': he was more than ready to share the credit with a man he so enormously admired. But he was a poet, not a philosopher. Nor, according to philosophers, was Bolingbroke: both, like Swift, suspected all 'systems'.

At all events Pope knew what he was about in writing this poem: it is grand, it is thoughtful, but it is also full of humour:

> Know Nature's children shall divide her care;
> The fur that warms a monarch warm'd a bear.
> While man exclaims, 'See all things for my use!'
> 'See man for mine,' replies a pamper'd goose . . .

with other amusing observations here and there to humble human pride. But all the while, Pope was aware that he was making an important statement, and he was a little frightened to think that his 'optimistic' philosophy, 'Whatever is is right,' might not be altogether orthodox. He discreetly published the first Epistle anonymously, and then anxiously waited to see what his steady old conscience, John Caryll, would have to say about it. His letters to Caryll at this time in themselves constitute a delicious Meredithian comedy: Pope is always being such a good boy! And Pope, although he was a free enough thinker, was loyal to his Church: he did not want to be thought a bad Catholic. Bolingbroke had told him: 'I know your precaution enough to know that you will screen yourself [in the generalities of poetry] against any direct charge of heterodoxy.' But Pope was a little uneasy about it. 'The town,' he wrote to Caryll on March 8th, 1733,

is now very full of a poem entitled *An Essay on Man*, attributed, I
think with reason, to a divine. It has merit in my opinion, but not
so much as they give it. At least it is incorrect, and has some in-
accuracies in the expressions – one or two of an unhappy kind, for
they may cause the author's sense to be turned, contrary to what
I think his intention, a little unorthodoxically.

There was, as he warned Caryll, an *if* instead of a *since* that
might 'overthrow his meaning', and he was referring to:

> If to be perfect in a certain state,
> What matter here or there, or soon or late,

as though immortality were conjectural. Again the lines –
he did not quote them, he merely referred to them:

> All are but parts of one stupendous whole,
> Whose body Nature is, and God the Soul;

'at the first glance may be taken for heathenism'; and indeed, at the second or third glance there is no reason to think
that they might not have been written by any religiously-
minded pagan. On October 23rd he tells Caryll, 'I believe
the author of the Essay on Man will end his poem in such a
manner as will satisfy your scruple': and on New Year's
Day 1734: 'To the best of my judgement the author shows
himself a Christian at last . . . ' though the 'assertion' on
which the claim is based is as much Platonic as anything
else. But then, as Bolingbroke had told him, 'In natural
religion the clergy are unnecessary, in revealed they are
dangerous guides'.

Caryll (who died in 1736) appears to have been satisfied
in the end, but not so some others, notably, in 1737–8, a
Swiss pastor called Crousaz, who in refuting the *Essay*,
found all sorts of heresies in it, accusing Pope of Spinozism,
and other dubious, not to say heathenish doctrines. This
was very worrying to Pope, for the time had passed when

you could be openly unbelieving; and besides, Pope, in what might be called a rather broad way, did hold the Christian beliefs, though he disliked dogma. Grub-Street of course attacked him, and he was altogether very uneasy till a rescuer appeared. This was William Warburton, a dull, heavy, ambitious, bullying man, whom nobody seems much to have liked while he lived, and most have contemptuously loathed since he died. He began life as an attorney's clerk and ended as a Bishop. Having at one time condemned the *Essay*, in 1738, irritated by Crousaz, he began to defend it, and did this so well (at least he said that there was nothing in it inconsistent with Christianity) that Pope fell into his arms; and after meeting him in 1740 established him as a kind of protector. Which was a pity, because after Pope died, this leaden-minded man became the official guardian of Pope's memory and works, ousting the amiable and sensitive but too modest Spence, who would have done it all so much better.

VIII

GATHERING UP THE THREADS

Y ET busy as Pope was during this decade, with his poetry,
his friends, and his garden, he found time for another
furious activity which stretched his ingenuity to the utmost.
This was the publication of his letters, an affair of such
intricacy, subterfuge, double-dealing and laying of false
trails, that it is unlikely that we shall ever know the complete truth about it. The whole business is clamorously
comic, and a little pitiable.

The story begins in 1727, when that faithful enemy
Curll published the correspondence between Pope and
Cromwell, which Cromwell had given to his mistress, and
which the latter when out of funds had sold to Curll for ten
pounds. This in one way was very annoying: nobody likes to
have his juvenilia laid open to the eye of any fool, all the
sillinesses of adolescence, all the things he wishes he hadn't
said, their fatuity, pomposity, and here and there, perhaps,
their indecorum. On the other hand, of course, it is rather
nice to feel that you are so interesting that someone thinks
it worth while to publish your letters, and others find them
worth while reading and buying. So when in 1728 Wycherley's posthumous remains were given to the public, Pope, to
justify his old friend, as he said (though in fact nothing of

the sort was involved) printed his correspondence with Wycherley. They were after all, he thought, rather good letters, though a little stilted and affected. And so, what with one consideration and the other, at about this time Pope thought it as well to call in his correspondence, and to write round to such of his friends as he thought might have kept his letters, so that they should be under his hand. Many of them complied, though some with a good deal of reluctance, as for example Caryll, who had transcripts made before returning them, for which posterity owes him a great debt.

And if you are going to collect your letters, and they are likely some day to be published, it is obviously just as well that they should come out under your eye. So Pope decided to publish – and edit – his letters. But 'The Letters of Alexander Pope' were not going to be just a collection of scraps of writing various occasions had called forth. They would be characteristic of his mind, they would be a mirror of all that had been best in his life. After all, what the world ought to have was a portrait – that is to say a work of art, an idealization – of a great poet, which should also in part be a biography and a justification. So when he had got them together, he destroyed a certain number (he said he burnt three-quarters of them), re-wrote and polished some, altered the date where it seemed convenient, and in some cases re-addressed them. For instance, there were hardly any letters to Addison. Now he had known Addison fairly well at one time; he must have written to Addison, the public would expect some letters to Addison – they would be part of the picture – so as there were more Caryll letters than necessary, he placed a few to Addison's address. And so on.

He has been very much blamed for this, scorned, reviled

and lashed. But after all, few people would like the whole of their letters published, with the hundred regrettable stupidities they have uttered. His action did nobody any harm. What it did do was to present an idealized Pope whom everybody would revere and love, an almost faultless man. That to-day we think rather silly. Who would wish to be faultless? We would be more cynical in preparing our letters for posterity, and say: 'Oh well, that is the sort of person I was,' as though we had given up the unequal contest with virtue. Moreover, in one sense, there was nothing dishonest in what Pope did: he wasn't making a statement before a court of law, but was presenting a work of literature, as much part of his Works as a poem. In those days letters were largely regarded as such – were there not the Letters of Voiture which everybody admired so much? It seems a little monkey-like to us: the trick was not wicked, it was only mischievous.

There was, however, a difficulty. To publish your own letters was not quite the right thing. To do so would smack of vanity, inordinate vanity. Pope therefore had to find someone to publish the letters for him, or else find an excuse for publishing them himself. He did both. His method was ingenious and complicated. Having 'edited' his letters, he made a careful copy, and deposited them all in the library of his friend Lord Oxford. Now for the excuse – which had obviously to be a pirated, and therefore supposedly inaccurate, edition. Who was going to produce this? And how was he to 'steal' the letters? Curll, the white-faced, goggle-eyed, splay-footed old enemy was the obvious man, so accordingly in 1733 a mysterious person signing himself 'P.T.' wrote to Curll offering to sell him a large number of Pope letters in his possession, provided Curll would publish an advertisement saying that he had the originals. Curll was no fool;

he wasn't going to convict himself of theft, so fought shy till March 1735, when he wrote to Pope suggesting they should call all their wars off, and sending him a copy of the suggested advertisement. This was so much what Pope wanted, that it may be that one of his 'scavengers' (such as he had employed for the *Dunciad* and still did for the *Grub-Street Journal*) had suggested it to Curll. Pope at once published the whole story, said he knew nothing of P.T., believed the letters to be forgeries, and washed his hands of the whole business. P.T. then told Curll, who was enraged by the rebuff, that he possessed printed sheets of the letters: negotiations went on, and soon a 'short, squat' emissary of P.T. who called himself Smythe, and wore a parson's clothes with a barrister's bands, came with some of the sheets. Curll then published.

Pope raised a terrible outcry. Curll was summoned before the Lords on the ground that there was a letter to a peer (there was in some of the earlier sheets) and altogether there was a terrific to-do. But the more fuss Pope made, the more it became clear to anyone interested that Pope had 'stolen' the letters himself, and that the spare offprints of the Wycherley letters that were used were those that Pope had himself bought from the printer when they did not sell, that in short the whole thing was an elaborate plot he had contrived, so as to make it only right in self-defence to publish his own edition of his letters. The odd thing is, that nobody seemed to mind. The letters were acclaimed; everybody said what a great and good man Mr Pope must be: and among them was the great 'good man' of the time, Ralph Allen, the original of Fielding's Squire Allworthy. So no harm was done. And in 1737 Pope, perhaps with some reluctance, published his own 'authoritative' edition, with texts tactfully revised. But, having made a clear difference

between his edition and Curll's, in later versions he tended
to reprint the texts of 1735 rather than those of 1737.

But neither contained his correspondence with Swift, nor
those charming letters that he, together with Bolingbroke
and Gay, had written to Swift. He had some time earlier
suggested to the Dean that the letters ought to be made
safe, preferably by sending them to him; but Swift had
taken no action. The Curll edition of 1735 made Pope renew
his plea: the letters might be stolen and falsified. Swift told
Pope to have no fear: he would burn the letters. This would
never do! Pope then very honestly said that he would like to
have their correspondence published as an honour to himself; but the idea did not amuse Swift, and it was only after
a great deal of trouble, and with the help of Swift's house-
keeper-cousin, Mrs Whiteway, and his new young friend,
the nice if rather stupid Lord Orrery, that Pope was able to
get the letters. But if Pope had them, he was shy of publishing them himself; someone else must do it. So he had a
secret edition printed, and a copy sent to Swift with an
anonymous letter suggesting that it would be a great pity
to suppress it, and asking Swift himself to publish the
collection. Poor Swift, now beginning to fail, a little
flurried by all this pother, but quite awake to the sort of
thing that was going on (he was himself an unblushing
trickster in publication) filled in a few of the names, and
sent the copy to his publisher, Faulkner, with orders to
print.

Mrs Whiteway, however, was uneasy. Would Faulkner,
she asked, first find out what Pope's wishes were? and
Faulkener, being a decent man, knowing also that Swift was
no longer quite responsible, agreed to ask Pope. This was
most annoying. Pope of course had to say 'no' to the publication, but he kept his letter back a month in the hope that

Faulkner would not wait. But Faulkener did wait. Pope then said he would like to have a chance of seeing what the letters were, and asked Orrery to look through them to decide whether they should be allowed to go forward: he didn't know what stuff a 'confederacy of people' in London might be putting over on to the public. Orrery looked over the letters, and then most irritatingly said that he didn't think they were worth publishing. Worse and worse! What was Pope to do? He wanted the letters published, but he didn't want to seem to publish them himself. The only possible thing was to take the line that, as the letters were there somebody would certainly print them; and as this would please Swift, things being as they were, Faulkener had better carry on; but he himself would have nothing to do with so horrid an affair. So the letters were published in Dublin as 'a reprint', Faulkner – the stubborn man would not play the game – declining to say that they were issued on the sole authority of the Dean.

All this fuss and bother seems almost incomprehensible to us: it was all part of the defence mechanism which was never quiet in Pope. If he published himself he would lay himself open to the imputation of vanity, and it might all be very disagreeable. At any rate the correspondence is in itself delightful, however garbled it may be. Much, of course, is not touched, and such events as the coming to light of the Caryll copies has enabled later editors to restore greater verity to the volumes. The early letters it is true are stilted and affected in manner. Pope was writing epistolary essays, as was to some extent the fashion. As he grew older he abandoned artifice, and wrote as it came to him to put things down as a trained writer may. His are not the most natural letters in the collection – those of Arbuthnot must claim that place – but they read evenly with those of Caryll

and Bolingbroke and Swift and Gay. The styles vary: Pope's
own style alters according to the recipient of the letter, as
any sensible man's does: after all, we write for the pleasure
of the person we are writing to, not for our own. But cavil
as we may, it remains true that no one can read the letters
which passed between the people named above without
realizing that he is in the presence of very great men.

By 1740, Pope was beginning to feel that his activities,
and perhaps his life, were drawing to a close. Most of his
old cronies were dead – all his friends and patrons of the
early days of the century, and lately Congreve, Gay,
Arbuthnot – while Swift was no longer in possession of his
senses, and Bolingbroke was largely abroad. He felt it was
time to gather up what was left of his poetical schemes, and
put together what among his old papers might be of use.
The first thing was to collect what he could of the *Memoirs
of the Extraordinary Life Works and Discoveries of Martinus Scriblerus*, which though old stuff, and to some extent
work by the old group, he partly re-wrote, and thoroughly
reorganized. It is, of its kind, inimitably good: but its kind
will appeal only to the specialist, and the historian of ideas.
More important for Pope – and for us – was his handling of
the grandiose scheme of didactic poetry of which the *Essay
on Man* and the *Moral Essays* were all that had been done.
Pope no longer felt equal to the whole task. Instead he gave
the world, in 1742, *The New Dunciad: As it was found in
the Year* 1741.

This poem, though it now forms Book IV of *The Dunciad*,
is quite different in tone from the earlier production. Pope
is no longer attacking individual dunces, but the whole
social scene: it is much more generalized in its satire, and it
includes some of the subjects he had intended to treat of in
the Ethic Epistles, such as education. It is a magnificent pro-

test against limitation and corruption, an argument in favour of all that is vital, an attack on all that is negative or distorted. The gravamen of the charge against educationists is when they proudly declare:

> Plac'd at the door of Learning, youth to guide,
> We never suffer it to stand too wide:

that against virtuoso scientists when the Goddess of Dullness exclaims:

> O! would the Sons of Men once think their Eyes
> And Reason giv'n them but to study *Flies*!
> See Nature in some partial narrow shape,
> And let the Author of the Whole escape:

the Book being in its structure made to dance with delightful movement full of bubbling humour to give buoyancy to the weighty accusations of futility in many forms – the Grand Tour, the Italian Opera, and so on. There is the famous pun about wandering in the Cambridge Colleges,

> Where Bentley late tempestuous wont to sport
> In troubled waters, but now sleeps in Port,

and here and there are couplets of grave lyric beauty, as:

> To where the Seine, obsequious as she runs,
> Pours at great Bourbon's feet her silken sons:

or the well-known paragraph imitatively describing the flutterings of the butterfly pursued by the collector. These are brilliant evocations: and the last paragraph of the old third Book was re-written to conclude the triumphant fourth, the tremendous vision of Night Primeval ending:

> Lo! thy dread Empire, CHAOS! is restor'd
> Light dies before thy uncreating word:
> Thy hand, great Anarch! lets the curtain fall,
> And Universal Darkness buries All.

a passage which even those hostile to Pope and his art admit to be great poetry. The word 'uncreating' is the key to the whole work.

The new poem would naturally be embodied in a complete *Dunciad*, towards which Pope was revising his earlier text in anticipation of the year 1743, when the copyright would revert to him by the original agreement with the publisher. He would be free to make what changes he liked, and the greatest would be that Theobald would almost disappear – he was a friend of Warburton's – and Cibber would be enthroned in his place. Pope had for a long time been on bad terms with Cibber, ever since the *Three Hours after Marriage* imbroglio: moreover Cibber had consistently despised and even maltreated his friends; Rowe, for instance: he had insultingly refused Fenton's *Mariamne*, which had been a success at the rival theatre, and had timidly rejected Gay's *Beggar's Opera*. What, however, more especially qualified Cibber for the elevation to monarchy in the *Dunciad* was the fact that since the first edition he had been made Poet Laureate – inditing the most villainous birthday odes – and had written a gossipy *Apology* which Pope despised, though we now find it vivid, racy, and alive with the sense of its time. Now, the rumour of his probable elevation having got abroad, he tried to prevent it by publishing in 1742 *A Letter from Mr Cibber to Mr Pope*. It is in many ways a good letter, as part of the war of the dunces and the Grub-Street campaign it is a lively document; in particular, when referring to Pope's furious indignation whenever his work was criticised, Cibber very sensibly remarks 'You seem in your *Dunciad*, to have been angry at the rain for wetting you, why then would you go into it? You could not but know that an Author, when he publishes a Work, exposes himself to all weathers'. Perfectly true, so doubly irritating. But, what was inexcusably gross, he told a story of an escapade when Pope was a very innocent young man about town, and no better in his morals than other young sparks of those days, an escapade in which Cibber and Lord Warwick, after a hilarious evening with Pope, had dragged him off to a 'house of carnal recreation', and exposed his absurd frame to ridicule. The story was brutally told; and immediately there leaped out from the press a number of hideous caricatures, and jeering verses which have caused this to be known as the tom-tit episode. It was a horribly humiliating stroke to deal a man of Pope's age and standing – this confrontation of his dignified age with a grim mockery of his silly youth. It is a tribute to his indomitable courage that he did not stay his hand or writhe helplessly under the blow, but went serenely on, gathered his energies, and in 1743, printed the new version. It was his last publication.

EPILOGUE

No one contemplating the convincingly expressive bust that Roubilliac made of Pope in 1738 (now at Temple Newsam), can fail to be charmed by the tremulous modelling of the cheek, the delicate sensuousness of the mouth, framed though it is in lines of suffering. But, he will ask, is there not some hint, somewhere, of combativeness? It is not in the beautiful calm line of the forehead, nor in the thoughtful eyes; the long, shapely nose, seems even in marble to quiver with sensibility. Yet is there not something in the way it is set, about the slight curve at the bridge, that reveals, or at least arouses suspicions of – aggressiveness?

Such a quality was perhaps a condition of Pope's survival; for mere resignation to the disgrace of his physical being would not have been enough to make his life bearable. Unable to get up or go to bed by himself, strapped up by day in a stiff canvas bodice to keep his frame straight – it wasted on one side – wearing three pairs of stockings to make his calves look even decently reputable, so easily chilled that he wore a kind of fur doublet beneath a thick linen shirt, and constantly racked by headaches, it is amazing that he should have carried his four foot six of humped humanity with so much cheerfulness, good temper, and benevolence. The fiery bright and dauntless spirit had of necessity to oppose itself actively to fat ease and complacency, to intellectual sloth, or dullness of physical perception; for the sake of its very self, attack the men who harboured these negations.

Regarding him as a social being apart from his existence as an author ('Heaven! was I born for nothing but to write?'), you are drawn to dwell upon his virtues; first his obvious goodnesses, his help to the struggling – to Savage, for example, and even to Dennis in his aged indigence; his innumerable kindnesses to little people, involving a great deal of trouble; his giving more than a tenth of his income to charity, his kindness to wearisome authors whose works he read and improved – however much he might bemoan it in the 'Prologue to the Satires' – and then you think of something more difficult, his virtue as a companionable human being. Moreover the kind of portent that he was entailed another kind of virtue: he had worked indefatigably to make himself independent; he never had to sell or hire his pen, never write a word he did not want to write, and he was the first author to live by his profession without adulation or fawning or parasitism. He transformed the social position of the man of letters, not because he himself, of comparatively humble origin, came to mix on level terms with the great landed aristocracy, but because he established for the writer a definite place in society: yet he found time to be the warmest-hearted of human beings in daily life. An early essay in the *Guardian* (No. 61) 'Against Barbarity to Animals' is one of the earliest of statements of humanitarianism (he was closely followed in this by James Thomson), and it was perhaps his own physical weakness, combined with immense nervous vitality, that gave him his deep sympathy with all living things. His fondness for dogs was notorious. His own Great Dane, Bounce, was one of the great pleasures and cares of his life – an intelligent creature who wrote an admirable poem to Lady Suffolk's lap-dog, Fop; and if kept in her kennel too long, she would when let out leap exuberantly upon Pope and roll him over. A surprising picture! And it was because of his weakness, perhaps, that he liked people who had in them abundance of life, of positive life, of natural goodness as with Bethel and Allen, of large-hearted vitality as in the far from virtuous Bathurst, of intellectual vitality as in his literary friends: the other side of the medal was his striking out viciously, almost you might think with the virulence of fear, at those who opposed life, who lessened its stream, who denied what was positive, pretenders to virtues they had not got.

It is pleasant to think of him in the more genial moments of his life, say at Twickenham in 1726, when, as Bolingbroke reminded him, he sauntered alone with the fallen statesman, 'or, as we have often done, with good Arbuthnot, and the jocose Dean of St Patrick's, among the multiplied scenes of your little garden.' It is when he could enjoy 'the feast of reason and the flow of soul,' that he was most himself, whether at his own home entertaining in house or grotto, or with Jervas the painter in London, at Ladyholt with Caryll, or visiting his great friends at Stowe or Cirencester or Hagley, or perhaps steering the frail bark of his body to career at Bath with Gay. The amount of travel he did in his latter years was astonishing; he seems never to have been still, and though always visiting, ever writing. Yet while his mother lived he felt tied by her possible needs, and would never go away without consideration for her well-being.

But, as we have seen, in that decade other deaths made him lonelier, and his vigour began to ebb. He had indeed in fragmentary form a further Horatian poem, *One Thousand*

Seven Hundred and Forty, which he might finish – it would, of course, become something else – if death did not overtake him first. Of his old literary group none were left available to encourage and to laugh, their place being taken by the blundering but reassuring Warburton – the most impudent man alive, Bolingbroke called him – who usurped the place posterity would wish Spence to have held. Added to his usual ills and ailments, asthma came to torture his nights still further. He had for years been an ill sleeper, declaring in his first satire:

> I think,
> And for my soul, I cannot sleep a wink.
> I nod in company, I wake at night,

and indeed he carried nodding in company to such lengths that he slept when the Prince of Wales, then head of the opposition faction, came to dine, though it is only fair to add that Frederick was at the moment discoursing of poetry. The valetudinaire was, alas, no longer gay, but a trial to the servants of his friends, though those who looked after him had no cause to complain of his meanness. He came to rely more and more upon the presence of Martha Blount, and his eye would always light up when he saw her approach. She came indeed to figure more in his life than was agreeable to his friends, and when in 1743 together with Pope she visited the Allens at Prior Park, Mrs Allen as good as turned her out of the house. Perhaps she presumed too much; but after all, was anybody so devoted to Pope as she was? In revenge she was the cause of his 'polluting his will with female resentment' as regards the Allens.

It was in this year that he seems to have felt his end approaching, for he then made his will, leaving most of his goods to Martha Blount, and the copyright of his work to Warburton; as he broke up it was Bolingbroke and Marchmont who were his main contact with the outer world. 'Yes,' he wrote to them,

> I would see you as long as I can see you, and then shut my eyes upon the world as a thing worth seeing no longer. If your charity would take up a small bird that is half-dead of the forest, and set it a-chirping for half an hour, I will jump into my cage, and put myself into your hands to-morrow at any hour you send. Two horses will be enough to draw me (and two dogs if you had them).

About three weeks before he died he sent copies of his *Ethic Epistles* to his friends, commenting: 'Here I am, like Socrates, dispensing my morality amongst my friends just as I am dying'. He was serene enough, not doubting of a future existence, feeling the soul's immortality within him, 'as though by intuition'.

For the remainder of the time Bolingbroke and March-mont, together with the devoted Spence, were constantly with him, and 'it was very observable that Mrs Blount's coming in gave a new turn of spirits, or a temporary strength to him'. He gradually became ever more delirious or coma-tose, but always in his moments of recollection seemed anxious to say kind things about his friends. 'I never in my life,' Bolingbroke said, 'knew a man that had so tender a heart for his particular friends, or a more general friendship for mankind': and burst out, 'I have known Pope these thirty years, and value myself more in his friendship than . . . ' and could not go on. The day before he died he received extreme unction at the suggestion of a friend, not that he thought it essential, but that 'it would look right', a gesture Chesterfield regarded as sacrificing a cock to Aesculapius. He ended peacefully on May 30th, 1744, being a few days over fifty-six years old.

Looking back on Pope's life, we may well think that the most astonishing thing about it – apart always from his

dazzling accomplishment as a poet – is the tension at which
it was lived. Enormously loved and abundantly hated, his
own affections were devoted and profound, his hatreds
rabid and sometimes unreasonable. But how vividly every
moment of his life was experienced! With what fervour his
creative imagination raised every action, every incident, to
the height of significance! 'By turns we catch the vital
spark and die': and the portion that he caught seemed never
to dim during the tempestuous years that it blazed or
glowed, to fuse life in the crucible of art, or to warm and
illuminate his friends.

INDEX

INDEX